God Heard

31 Prayers that the Lord Heard
and I Overheard

Thomas E. Phillips

Acknowledgements

The ideas in this book flow from a thousand streams, many with names long forgotten by the author. However, I wish to offer particular thanks for four groups of people. First, I offer sincere thanks to my colleagues in ministry and in higher education who read early drafts of this work and who made helpful suggestions, most notably, Ev Leadingham, Tom Oord, Frank Carver, John Denney, Barry Callen, Dee Kelly, Chris Kohlbry, and Judi King. Their advice was deeply helpful. Second, I offer sincere appreciation to the friends in the Crosswalk Adult Bible Study who worked through many of these prayers with my co-teacher, Brad Kelle, and I. My experience with these fellow believers at San Diego First Church of the Nazarene has been profoundly gratifying over the last several years. Third, Norm Shoemaker and the students in Point Loma Nazarene University's Masters of Ministry were also kind enough to listen to my oral presentation of several of these prayers and their kind attention is also deeply appreciated. Finally, I wish to offer my highest thanks for Jordan Frye, who first suggested that I considered composing a volume like this. I am thankful for such a great cloud of witnesses.

Preface

As a university professor of theology, I work with hundreds o' Christians in their late teens and early twenties. Over the years, I've become convinced that there is one area where young Christians—and perhaps all Christians—encounter their greatest spiritua' disappointments and frustrations. That area is prayer. Ironically, the frustration that many people experience with prayer has little to do with God. People are seldom disappointed with God or with God's response to their prayers. Rather, people are often frustrated with themselves and disappointed by their own failure to establish and maintain a consistent prayer life.

Of course, young people are not the only people who struggle in their prayer lives. *Can you imagine any of the Christians that you know saying something like "Man, I've gotta cut back on my prayer life" or "you know, I'm spending way too much time with the Lord"?* Of course not, the truth is that when most of us hear sermons on prayer, it's easy to make us feel guilty about not praying enough.

As a teen, I once attended a prayer meeting where we went around the room and had each person pray aloud for a few minutes. Most of us had been attending church for years and so we were comfortable praying with our friends. I happened to pray first that night. So, I prayed for a few minutes, and said "amen." Then I waited for the girl on my left to begin praying. For what seemed like an eternity, nothing happened. Then, in a voice only slightly above a whisper, she said, "Lord, help the people in the hospitals and stuff Amen."

At first, several of us felt embarrassed for this young lady who apparently didn't know how to pray. But within a few minutes, most o' us became ashamed of ourselves both for judging her and for embarrassing her. She had only been a Christian for a few weeks and no one had ever taught her how to pray. I think that day was the first time that I began to think about *the importance of overheard prayers.* I think that this book has grown out of those awkward experiences more than thirty years ago. I have become convinced that people who know how to pray only know how to pray because they have overheard the prayers of others.

That's what this little book is about—overheard prayers. Most but not all of these prayers, come from the Bible. Many of the prayers are quite well known; a few may not be familiar. These prayers vary widely. They come from sinners and saints; some offer hope and some reek of desperation. Some express an extraordinary faith through beautiful poetry and some bellow out desperate and even ill-considered words. *These prayers vary in content, tone and purpose; they have two things in common—God heard them and I have overheard them.*

I have often had the experience of hearing a fellow believer pray and of sensing that she or he had just put into words exactly what I was feeling at that moment but could not express. *This book is a collection of those experiences, the overheard prayers that have allowed me to borrow a brother or sister's faith, to participate in their loneliness, to learn from their devotion, to be inspired by their praise, to feel their pain, to glow in their heart's aspiration, or to join in their repentance.*

Over the years, I have become convinced of these two things—that God hears and even appreciates every prayer and that I have been enriched by nearly every prayer that I have ever overheard. It is my prayer that your Christian life will likewise be enriched as you overhear these overheard prayers.

Finally, I have provided prayers from several different Biblical translations (NIV, TNIV, NAB, NASB, ESV, NKJV, RSV, NRSV, etc.). When Biblical prayers are not attributed to a particular translation, the translation is my own.

Contents

Prayers of Daily Life

Each of these first three prayers have been recited by Christians for millennia (the Lord's Prayer), for centuries (the Prayer of St. Francis), or for decades (the Serenity Prayer). I and millions of other Christians have found each prayer helpful in teaching us how to pray. These prayers speak to our shared experiences and common concerns. I offer these prayers and my brief comments on them as primers for your daily experience in prayer.

1

The Lord's Prayer

Our Father who is in heaven,
Hallowed be your name.
Your kingdom come,
Your will be done
on earth as it is in heaven.
Give us this day our daily bread
And forgive us our trespasses
As we forgive those who trespass against us
And lead us not into temptation,
But deliver us from evil.
For yours is the kingdom and the power and the glory forever.
Amen
Matthew 6:9-13

Any collection of prayers must begin here. This is the model prayer that Jesus gave his disciples when they asked him to teach them how to pray. As I have quoted it, the prayer is a modernized version of the prayer preserved in the King James Version of Matthew's Gospel (6:9-13), but the prayer exists in many versions. Most contemporary English translations omit the last sentence from the prayer because most ancient copies of Matthew's Gospel don't include this last sentence. An even shorter version of the prayer exists in Luke's Gospel (11:2-4). Another very early Christian text, the *Didache* (8:2), also contains a very similar version of this prayer and instructs its readers to recite this prayer three times each day (8:3).

I first read the *Didache* and its instructions for Christians to say this prayer three times daily while I was sitting in a university library just over twenty years ago. I remember that day well because I paused and recited this prayer for the first time that afternoon. I have prayed this prayer three times nearly every day since then.

I'm sure that I haven't learned everything that this prayer has to teach, but my time with this prayer has taught me a few things. First, *if I want to understand what this world should be like, I have to look beyond it.* There is a place—heaven—where God dwells and where the Father's will is done. If the places of my life are ever to look like that place, that miracle will come only through prayer.

Second, *I am privileged.* I've never been really hungry, at least not to the point of true bodily distress. I've never seen a day without bread, but other people have. If you're privileged like me and you pray "give us our daily bread" three times each day, wait and see what happens. I bet you'll *become uncomfortably aware of two things, that you already have all the bread that you really need and that Christ calls us to help those who do not.*

Third, *the more that I plead for forgiveness, the easier it is to forgive.* When someone—even a guy like me—pleads for forgiveness three times a day, something wonderful happens. A genuine, kind and loving, spirit of forgiveness wells up naturally in the heart of the truly forgiven. It's hard to remain unforgiving when you thrice daily pray, "forgive us our trespasses."

Finally, *the first step in overcoming temptation is avoiding temptation.* There are places I cannot comfortably go and things that I cannot really do while I am praying "lead us not into temptation." It's easier to avoid such places and activities when I sincerely pray this prayer. These words lead me away from temptation. It's probably significant that the prayer does not request the power to withstand temptation; the prayer requests the guidance to avoid temptation.

Lord, teach us to pray.

Prayer of St. Francis

Lord, make me an instrument of your peace.
Where there is hatred, let me sow love,
Where there is injury, pardon, Where there is doubt, faith,
Where there is despair, hope, Where there is darkness, light,
Where there is sadness, joy.
O Divine Master, grant that I may not so much
seek to be consoled as to console,
not so much to be understood as to understand,
not so much to be loved, as to love;
for it is in giving that we receive,
it is in pardoning that we are pardoned,
it is in dying that we awake to eternal life.

This moving prayer is attributed to St. Francis of Assisi (1182-1226). Even though we can't be certain that Francis penned these exact words, the prayer sounds consistent with what we know about St. Francis. He came from a wealthy and influential family, but he renounced his inherited wealth and privileges during his late teen years and took on a life of voluntary poverty. The Christian tradition is rich with stories of his kindness and humility. Because of his reported kindness to small animals, even now, nearly eight centuries after his death, many prayer gardens still contain statues of the saint with sparrows resting in his palms and chipmunks playing at his feet. St. Francis is one of the few people in history who is reported to have prayed so earnestly for Christlikeness that he began to bleed from his hands, feet, side, back and forehead just as Christ did on the cross. (This experience is called stigmata.)

This prayer is structured around three key ideas—*sowing, seeking, and receiving.* Sowing. Francis opened his prayer with a plea that he would become an instrument which sowed divine peace. The dusty and dirty character of the verb "sow" is important. Francis wanted to become an earthy "instrument." He neither

4

requested any special distinctions nor claimed any inherent rights. For the sake of divine service, *he asked only to become a lowly tool.* St. Francis pled for the humiliating privilege of initiating redemption and reconciliation in face of sin and disillusionment.

Seeking. Our world is often stalemated by conflict. Competing desires and escalating demands paralyze love and stifle compassion as each individual seeks his or her own advantage, each one desiring to gain something from the other. St. Francis's prayer turns this system upside down. He does not seek to gain advantage or to receive generosity. Rather, like a great physician, he seeks to distribute assistance and compassion. *While most people need to be appreciated, St. Francis prayed for the ability to appreciate.*

Receiving. One of the great and perplexing truths of the Christian faith—perhaps the central truth of the faith—is what some have called *the paradox of intentions. As strange as it sounds, the greatest accomplishments in life cannot be achieved, they can only be received.* True happiness can only be received—never taken or earned. If we seek satisfaction in the self indulgent way that the world does, we will never find it. Life and life more abundantly can only be poured into a vessel that has been emptied of selfish cravings. It is paradoxical—illogically but undeniably true—that the deepest rewards in life are only found by those who have no desire to gain those rewards for themselves. By grace, *they desire to serve, love and sacrifice for no other purpose than to please God.* It is people such as this—and only people such as this—who receive the deepest satisfactions in life. This is what I take to be the meaning of Christ's admonition that those who wish to have life must first give up their lives. This is a paradox made comprehensible only through prayer.

Lord, remake my heart so that I may be the agent of your love.

The Serenity Prayer

God grant me
The serenity to accept the things I cannot change,
The courage to change the things I can,
And the wisdom to know the difference.
Living one day at a time,
Enjoying one moment at a time,
Accepting hardship as the pathway to peace.
Taking, as He did, this sinful world as it is, not as I would have it.
Trusting that He will make all things right if I surrender to His will.
That I may be reasonably happy in this life,
And supremely happy with Him forever in the next.
Amen.

If any of you lacks wisdom, ask God who gives to everyone
generously without finding fault,
and wisdom will be given to you.
James 1:5

This well-known serenity prayer is attributed to the mid-twentieth century pastor and theologian, Reinhold Niebuhr. Niebuhr probably borrowed some of these ideas from earlier prayers, but he began reciting this form of the prayer in worship services during the 1930s. Times were tough for an inner city pastor in 1930s Detroit. The Great Depression slogged on throughout the entire decade. Niebuhr saw good, honest, and hard-working people lose everything—their jobs, their homes, and sometimes their hope. To make matters worse, America was heading toward another devastating war. When Niebuhr looked toward Europe, he was seized with horror over the rise of the Nazis and their hateful ideologies. When Niebuhr looked toward Asia, he was sickened by Japan's violence in China and Korea. The people he loved around Detroit were being crushed by economic collapse; the people he loved across the Atlantic and Pacific Oceans were being assaulted by political violence. Niebuhr's world was depressing—economic gloom at home and impending war abroad.

Each Sunday, Niebuhr, a young and energetic pastor, faced a congregation which was struggling against a daily onslaught of gut-wrenching domestic turmoil and heart-rending international violence. He preached... and he prayed this prayer. Time passed. Niebuhr began to teach theology, but still he prayed this prayer. World War II and the Holocaust ripped at the very heart of our common humanity. Niebuhr prayed this prayer. The Cold War and its insane race to build "better" and "better" bombs chipped away at a fragile post-war peace. Still, Niebuhr prayed this prayer. Wars in Korea and Vietnam slashed at all Niebuhr's fondest hopes for a lasting peace and a truly just world, but still he prayed this prayer.

Niebuhr was famous for what he called "Christian realism." *It was Christian in that it was rooted in the hope of the supreme happiness that God has in store for those with the moral courage to surrender to God's goodness*; God's will often prevails only through our determined embrace of avoidable hardships. *It was realistic in that it acknowledged that not all things can be changed at the moment of our choosing*; in a sinful world, some things must be patiently endured. Christian realism demanded both the humility to accept the world as it is and the courage to imagine the world as it could be.

When God offered Solomon whatever he asked for, Solomon chose wisdom—and God was pleased. Without wisdom, other gifts can become a curse. Without wisdom, a commitment to justice can be misshapen into the arrogance of self-righteousness, and without wisdom, great visions can shatter into resentful shards of disillusion. In the absence wisdom, an honest acknowledgement of our limitations can be warped into complicity with small-mindedness, and in the absence of wisdom, a prudent recognition of our inability to do all things can be squeezed into a pact with inactivity. *Wisdom is the one gift with the ability to save us from the undesired byproducts of our other gifts.* Only wisdom, wisdom from God, enables us to recognize when our steely courage is becoming foolhardiness and when our serene acceptance is degenerating into complacency. *Serenity to accept; courage to act; and wisdom to distinguish. For these, we pray daily.*

Lord, remove whatever of me stands between me and the gift of your wisdom.

Prayers of Dedication

The five prayers recited under this category come from sources as diverse of the Old Testament, the New Testament, a children's rhyme, and an ancient Jewish novel. Each dedicates (or rededicates) something to the Lord—a temple, a field, a life, a marriage. Some of these prayers (St. Steven's prayer and Solomon's dedication of the temple) are quite well known. Others (Tobiah's prayer) are barely known except among historians and theologians. I offer each prayer and my comments for your use in reflecting upon prayer as an act of dedication to God.

Solomon's Dedication of the Temple

*"O LORD, God of Israel, there is no God like you in heaven above or on earth below—you who keep your **covenant** of love with your servants who continue wholeheartedly in your way. You have kept your **promise** to your servant David my father; with your mouth you have **promised** and with your hand you have fulfilled it—as it is today.*

*"Now LORD, God of Israel, keep for your servant David my father the **promises** you made to him when you said, 'You shall never fail to have a man to sit before me on the throne of Israel, if only your sons are careful in all they do to walk before me as you have done.' And now, O God of Israel, let your word that you **promised** your servant David my father come true.*

*"But will God really dwell on earth? **The heavens, even the highest heaven, cannot contain you. How much less this temple I have built!** Yet give attention to your servant's prayer and his plea for mercy, O LORD my God. Hear the cry and the prayer that your servant is praying in your presence this day. May your eyes be open toward this temple night and day, this place of which you said, 'My Name shall be there,' so that you will hear the prayer your servant prays toward this place. Hear the supplication of your servant and of your people Israel when they pray toward this place. Hear from heaven, your dwelling place, and when you hear, forgive.*

*"**When a man wrongs his neighbor** and is required to take an oath and he comes and swears the oath before your altar in this temple, then hear from heaven and act. Judge between your servants, condemning the guilty and bringing down on his own head what he has done. Declare the innocent not guilty, and so establish his innocence.*

*"**When your people Israel have been defeated by an enemy** because they have sinned against you, and when they turn back to you and confess your name, praying and making supplication to you in this*

temple, then hear from heaven and forgive the sin of your people Israel and bring them back to the land you gave to their fathers.

"**When the heavens are shut up** and there is no rain because your people have sinned against you, and when they pray toward this place and confess your name and turn from their sin because you have afflicted them, then hear from heaven and forgive the sin of your servants, your people Israel. Teach them the right way to live, and send rain on the land you gave your people for an inheritance.

"**When famine or plague comes** to the land, or blight or mildew, locusts or grasshoppers, or when an enemy besieges them in any of their cities, whatever disaster or disease may come, and when a prayer or plea is made by any of your people Israel—each one aware of the afflictions of his own heart, and spreading out his hands toward this temple—then hear from heaven, your dwelling place. Forgive and act; deal with each man according to all he does, since you know his heart (for you alone know the hearts of all men), so that they will fear you all the time they live in the land you gave our fathers.

"**As for the foreigner who does not belong to your people Israel but has come from a distant land because of your name**—for men will hear of your great name and your mighty hand and your outstretched arm—when he comes and prays toward this temple, then hear from heaven, your dwelling place, and do whatever the foreigner asks of you, so that all the peoples of the earth may know your name and fear you, as do your own people Israel, and may know that this house I have built bears your Name.

"**When your people go to war** against their enemies, wherever you send them, and when they pray to the LORD toward the city you have chosen and the temple I have built for your Name, then hear from heaven their prayer and their plea, and uphold their cause.

"**When they sin against you**—for there is no one who does not sin— and you become angry with them and give them over to the enemy, who takes them captive to his own land, far away or near; and if they have a change of heart in the land where they are held captive, and repent and plead with you in the land of their conquerors and

say, 'We have sinned, we have done wrong, we have acted wickedly';
and if they turn back to you with all their heart and soul in the land of
their enemies who took them captive, and pray to you toward the
land you gave their fathers, toward the city you have chosen and the
temple I have built for your Name; then from heaven, your dwelling
place, hear their prayer and their plea, and uphold their cause. And
forgive your people, who have sinned against you; forgive all the
offenses they have committed against you, and cause their
conquerors to show them mercy; for they are your people and your
inheritance, whom you brought out of Egypt, out of that iron-
smelting furnace.
"May your eyes be open to your servant's plea and to the plea of your
*people Israel, and may you listen to them **whenever they cry out to***
***you**. For you singled them out from all the nations of the world to be*
your own inheritance, just as you declared through your servant
Moses when you, O Sovereign LORD, brought our fathers out of
Egypt."
1 Kings 8:23-53 (New International Version)

I've seen a lot of things dedicated—everything from buildings and highways to monuments and babies—and I've noticed that dedications seem to be about *gratitude and resolve*. Gratitude? Who hasn't sat in a park next to a statue dedicated to a fallen hero or visited a sick friend in a hospital wing dedicated to a major donor? Resolve? Who hasn't worshipped in a church dedicated to the glory of God or studied in an academic building dedicated to the pursuit of knowledge? *Appreciation for services rendered, honor for sacrifices made, announcements of lofty purposes, and proclamations of noble intentions—these are the raw materials for a proper dedication.*

This prayer—one of the longest prayers in Scripture—has all the gratitude that we would expect from a major league dedication. Solomon has just built the first permanent temple ever built to honor God—a temple that his father David had been forbidden to build—and yet, remarkably, Solomon didn't even mention the temple in the first five sentences of this prayer. Instead, *Solomon used these first five sentences of his prayer to express his gratitude for God's covenant and promises.* Five times in five sentences Solomon extolled the wonder of God's covenant and God's promises. God's people had longed for a temple for so many generations, and Solomon had finally built it. Yet Solomon understood that the temple which he had built was proof of God's faithfulness—not Solomon's. *If we are ever truly to dedicate anything to God, our dedication must flow from deeply felt gratitude to God for the gifts and faithfulness of God.*

After praising God's faithfulness so fully, Solomon finally got around to mentioning the temple that he had built. But even then, Solomon's first reference to the temple was a simple acknowledgement that the temple had not trapped or contained God. Solomon's God could not be manipulated or coerced by human activity. We all know that nothing we create—not even our prayers—can box in God. However, when our desires are intense, we can easily fall prey to the subtle delusion that our prayers have obligated God to fulfill our designs and intentions. Solomon's prayer reminds us that God cannot be constrained to fit within even our most well-intentioned plans. We can set aside and dedicate space—both literal and metaphoric—for God in our world, but we cannot limit God to that space.

If Solomon's prayer fit into the typical gratitude/resolve pattern of dedications, we would expect Solomon's prayer to start emphasizing the people's resolve at this point. However, Solomon's prayer moves in a very different direction. *The final two-thirds of the prayer offer no declarations of the people's noble and unwavering resolve.* Instead, the prayer speaks of the people's inevitable failures, impending disasters, and unavoidable tragedies. Solomon's prayer anticipates hardships from without (defeats, droughts, famines, plagues, wars) and failures from within (sins and wrongs). Solomon didn't expect any fairy tale endings. He knew that difficulties would come and that human resolve would be insufficient to sustain the community. Solomon had no time for false bravo or for naïve confidence in the steadfastness of the human will.

Solomon understood that human will fails; mere human resolve cannot empower the people of God for the work of God. The best intentions and noblest desires of our race are no match for the vicissitudes of time. *Normally when we dedicate something, we call upon our deepest human resolve. Solomon's dedication called upon a deeper resolve—the faithfulness of God.*

Solomon's prayer should teach us at least one essential lesson: When believers dedicate themselves or their creations to God, they cannot call upon their own discipline, self-determination, or will power. Instead, believers must abandon their wills to the unwavering resolve of God to forgive, redeem and sustain the people of God. We seek to live in constant gratitude to our God who has resolved to save us.

Lord, teach me to bask in your faithfulness.

St. Stephen's Prayer
& the Child's Bedtime Prayer

"Lord Jesus, receive my spirit."
Acts 7:59

Now, I lay me down to sleep.
I pray the Lord my soul to keep.
If I die before I wake,
I pray the Lord my soul to take.

To many, the pairing of these prayers may seem strange. They are the final words of St. Stephen, the first martyr in the history of the Church, and the words of an easily memorized children's poem. Yet the two prayers are united by their shared confrontation with the advancing forces of death. Within moments of saying this prayer, Stephen died. His body being broken by the stones of a hateful mob. Stephen's death was horrible in its violence and senseless in its origin, making Stephen's prayer both desperate in its tone and eloquent in its simplicity.

Being designed to usher in a child's peaceful slumber, the children's prayer is more solemn than desperate. Yet, this children's prayer is also eloquent in its simplicity (notice that only one word contains more than one syllable). Still, whether solemn or desperate, both prayers are about preparing for death, that last foe of the saints.

I don't like thinking or talking about death. Over the years, I've lost many loved ones—neighbors, friends, classmates, even my father. Death is real to me. My high school friend Steve is dead; we will not play tennis together again on this earth. My father is dead; we will never again camp together in the rolling hills of the Midwest. Death is real to me. Still, for me, prayer is usually about the future— and about my future in this world. *Yet, this children's prayer—in*

15

fact, neither of these prayers—is about the future. They are about the end.

As a young father, I found this children's prayer particularly disturbing. I used to wonder why anyone would want to frighten their children by talking about death every night ("if I die before I wake"). I once heard a famous theologian ask a crowd of people how they wanted to die. Nearly everyone said that they wanted to die peacefully in their sleep. The theologian then read an eleventh century prayer to us that said, "God, save us from a sudden death." I—and most of those in the room—recognized this as a common line from ancient prayers, but the speaker reminded us of what we had conveniently forgotten—the ancients feared a sudden death because a sudden death would give them no time to prepare for death. Then, the theologian made a painful observation—*the ancients feared God, we fear death.*

What have I gained from these prayers? Maybe just this, *the ultimate purpose of prayer is to prepare us for our sure and impending death.*

Lord, teach me to live so that I may die well.

Jeremiah's Field

"Ah, Sovereign LORD, you have made the heavens and the earth by your great power and outstretched arm. Nothing is too hard for you. You show love to thousands but bring the punishment for the parents' sins into the laps of their children after them. Great and mighty God, whose name is the LORD Almighty, great are your purposes and mighty are your deeds. Your eyes are open to the ways of all; you reward everyone according to their conduct and as their deeds deserve. You performed signs and wonders in Egypt and have continued them to this day, both in Israel and among all nations, and have gained the renown that is still yours. You brought your people Israel out of Egypt with signs and wonders, by a mighty hand and an outstretched arm and with great terror. You gave them this land you had sworn to give their ancestors, a land flowing with milk and honey. They came in and took possession of it, but they did not obey you or follow your law; they did not do what you commanded them to do. So you brought all this disaster on them.
"See how the siege ramps are built up to take the city. Because of the sword, famine and plague, the city will be given into the hands of the Babylonians who are attacking it. What you said has happened, as you now see. And though the city will be given into the hands of the Babylonians, you, Sovereign LORD, say to me, 'Buy the field with silver and have the transaction witnessed.' "
Jeremiah 32:17-25 (Today's New International Version)

      If you had overheard Jeremiah offer this prayer about 2,600 years ago, you probably would have thought that Jeremiah had gone nuts. By the time that Jeremiah prayed these words of dedication over his newly purchased field, he had been in the unpopular business of predicting Israel's destruction for years and years. The Jeremiah who prayed this dedication had taken his licks. No one wanted to believe Jeremiah's predictions of devastation. Kings had shredded his prophecies into little pieces and set them on fire;

priests had publicly denounced him as an enemy of the temple; and the pundits of his day had labeled him a "false prophet." For years, Jeremiah had told the ancient Jews that God would send the Babylonians to conquer their land, to destroy their temple, and to drag their kings into captivity. Now, Jeremiah was buying a field and dedicating it to God in this soon-to-be conquered territory.

Had Jeremiah changed his mind about the impending Babylonian threat? No! Jeremiah could see the siege ramps and he knew what they meant. Jerusalem would be handed over to the Babylonians. In fact, Jerusalem was teetering on the verge of destruction as Jeremiah plopped down his dough to buy his field. *Even as he signed the closing papers, Jeremiah insisted that Babylonian swords and battle axes would render his deed completely worthless within just a few days.* Then, why waste easily hidden silver buying land that would soon be distributed to the soldiers of a conquering army? Jeremiah's real estate investment wouldn't have made sense to any shekel wise investor. It was like buying season tickets on the fifty yard line after your team had already lost the play-offs.

Jeremiah was short term pessimistic and long term optimistic. In the short term, *Jeremiah knew as a prophetic certainty that Israel would be invaded, Jerusalem would be conquered, and the temple would be destroyed.* Jeremiah had long insisted that Israel's sin was great and that God's judgment was sure. Jeremiah doubted that inevitable judgment no more than he doubted the evening sunset—the sound of the approaching Babylonian chariots would provide the crescendo to God's judgment upon Israel. In the longer term, however, Jeremiah was optimistic.

Jeremiah was optimistic that God's mercy would ultimately prevail and that God's people would again come to possess their land. That's why Jeremiah purchased and dedicated a field that he himself would never actually possess. His purchase and dedication were acts of faith and symbols of his unshaken confidence in the persistence of divine mercy. Jeremiah's prayer surveyed the history of that mercy in the lives of his ancestors; it rehearsed the story of

God's continual faithfulness to God's people. God had delivered them from Egypt and God had given them a land. But the people had sinned and their judgment was imminent. Still, in spite of the siege ramps around them, Jeremiah knew that God's undaunted love for God's people would bring an unfaithful people back to God and back to the land.

Jeremiah's prayer is remarkable. Jeremiah didn't dedicate his field as a way to avoid, evade or circumvent God's judgment. Instead, Jeremiah dedicated his field as an expression of his confidence in God's saving mercy in spite of the judgment and devastation that our sins brings upon us. *Sincere rededication, as in Jeremiah's prayer, shouldn't be about trying to get off the hook for our sins; it should be about choosing to live so that God can return us to where we should have been all along.*

As I've prayed this prayer, I've come to believe this: When we sin, sin brings devastation. When we've seen enough devastation and we're ready to change, rededication doesn't often spare us from the immediate hardship and pain that comes with sin. Reformed drug addicts go through painful detox; repentant thieves often go to prison; and forgiven gluttons face difficult diets. *Renewed dedication seldom removes the siege ramps that our sins have built around. However, if we're willing to buy a field and to dedicate it with the long term in mind, God is always faithful to God's people.*

Lord, infuse me with the optimism of God's grace.

Tobiah's Wedding Prayer

*Tobiah arose from bed and said to his wife, "My love, get up.
Let us pray ..." She got up, and they started to pray ... He began with
these words:*
*"Blessed are you, O God of our fathers; praised be your name forever
and ever. Let the heavens and all your creation praise you forever.
You made Adam and you gave him his wife Eve to be his help and
support; and from these two the human race descended. You said, 'It
is not good for the man to be alone; let us make him a partner like
himself.' Now, Lord, you know that I take this wife of mine not
because of lust, but for a noble purpose. Call down your mercy on me
and on her, and allow us to live together to a happy old age." They
said together, "Amen, amen."*
Tobit 8:4-8 (New American Bible)

Unlike the other prayers in this collection, this prayer is neither in the Protestant Bible nor well-known. I chose this prayer because I know of no other prayer quite like it—the prayer of newlyweds celebrating the gift of marriage and asking God's blessing upon their lives together. Thus, the prayer can properly be seen as a honeymoon couple's prayer of dedication.

I took the prayer from an ancient Jewish novel called "Tobit." The prayer appears about half through the story, after Tobiah has fallen in love with his beautiful fiancé, Sarah. Earlier in the story, a prophet encouraged Tobiah and Sarah to marry, but only after warning them to pray for God's blessing before they began indulging in the joyful escapades of their honeymoon. In compliance with these instructions, Tobiah and Sarah offered this prayer. Thus, at this point in the story, Tobiah and Sarah are in their bedroom together and Sarah's parents have just left the room. This is the first time that the couple has been alone in this way and both are virgins. Finally, they are married and they are really excited about what is about to take place. With that background...

20

This prayer intrigues me in two very different ways. *On the level of human emotions, the prayer is honest.* As human beings, we have very intense sexual desires and Tobiah's prayer is saturated with allusions to those desires. Adam and Eve must have desired one another to create so many descendents; Tobiah and Sarah expect to create descendents through the same delightful process. Of course, neither Adam and Eve nor Tobiah and Sarah, were merely "hooking up" (for lust); they were joining together for what Tobiah called a noble purpose. That noble purpose certainly included becoming one flesh, but it was more than just having sex. Sarah and Tobiah committed to share their lives together into a happy old age (according to the novel, they eventually even raised seven children together). Tobiah's prayer shows us that our sexual urges and our legitimate fulfillment of those urges in marriage are entirely consistent with the good that God intended (even if we don't have a house full of children like Tobiah and Sarah). *Tobiah and Sarah undoubtedly said, "amen, amen" to this prayer with sex on their mind—and that human reality is not shameful or unwholesome.* Our sexuality is never to be despised; it is to be disciplined.

On the level of divine-human interaction, the prayer emphasizes the gifts of creation. Tobiah understood the human needs for partnership and for sex as one powerful aspect of that partnership. Tobiah recognized these needs as divinely decreed. Tobiah rejoiced that God had given him and Sarah to one another just as God gave Adam and Eve to one another. Of course, neither Tobiah nor Genesis said that it was evil for people to be alone (celibacy is not impossible!). However, both Tobiah and Genesis insist that men and women were made for one another; they are the Creator's gifts for one another. *God is to be praised for the gifts of marriage and of sex within marriage, but these gifts, like all gifts from God, should be dedicated back to God.*

As I said, the book of Tobit is an ancient novel and we don't know if these events really happened or not, but we can learn at least one lesson from this candid ancient prayer: *Sex is a gift from*

21

the Creator, but a gift meant to be dedicated back to God for the noble purpose of a loving marriage.

Lord, thank you for the gift of love; bless me with the gift of unwavering fidelity.

Prayers of Repentance

Each of the prayers recited under this category is taken from the Bible. Most of these prayers (particularly Psalm 51 and the prayers of the Pharisee and the tax collector) are quite familiar to Christians through their use in worship. Unfortunately, believers sometimes make the mistake of thinking about repentance only as an act which moves us into the Christian faith. However, it is better to think of repentance as an act which both moves us into—*and sustains us within*—the Christian faith. I offer these prayers and my brief comments for your cultivation of a life characterized by repentance.

"David's" Prayer of Repentance (Ps 51)

Have **mercy** upon me, O God, according to Your **loving kindness;**
According to the multitude of Your **tender mercies,**
blot out my **transgressions.**
Wash me thoroughly from my **iniquity,**
and cleanse me from my **sin.**
For I acknowledge my transgressions,
and my sin is always before me.
Against You, You only, have I sinned,
and done this **evil** in Your sight—
That You may be found just when You speak,
and blameless when You judge.
Behold, I was brought forth in iniquity,
and in sin my mother conceived me.
Behold, You desire truth in the inward parts,
And in the hidden part You will make me to know wisdom.
Purge me with hyssop, and I shall be clean;
Wash me, and I shall be whiter than snow.
Make me hear joy and gladness,
that the bones You have broken may rejoice.
Hide Your face from my sins, and blot out all my iniquities.
Create in me a clean heart, O God,
and renew a steadfast spirit within me.
Do not cast me away from Your presence,
and do not take Your Holy Spirit from me.
Restore to me the joy of Your salvation,
and uphold me by Your generous Spirit.
Then I will teach transgressors Your ways,
and sinners shall be converted to You.
Deliver me from the guilt of bloodshed,
O God, the God of my salvation,
And my tongue shall sing aloud of Your righteousness.

O Lord, open my lips, and my mouth shall show forth Your praise.
For You do not desire sacrifice, or else I would give it;
You do not delight in burnt offering.
The sacrifices of God are a broken spirit,
a broken and a contrite heart—
These, O God, You will not despise.
Do good in Your good pleasure to Zion;
Build the walls of Jerusalem.
Then You shall be pleased with the sacrifices of righteousness,
With burnt offering and whole burnt offering;
Then they shall offer bulls on Your altar.
Psalm 51 (New King James Version)

We live in a therapy society. "Help" is a growth industry. Armies of smiling marketers cloak their sales pitches in the language of help. Need some help with your self-esteem, your acne, or your golf game? Help is just one 800 number away. Wordsmiths sit in cubicles and churn out slogans and clichés to reassure us that there's no shame in seeking help. Mantra after mantra is paraded before us, assuring us that "we all need a little help sometimes" and that "you can get the help you deserve." In our culture, no matter what your problem is, "help" is available. There's a cure for everything from troubled finances and absent romances to excess gas and thinning hair.

Unfortunately, people sometimes confuse the Biblical call for repentance with our culture's quick fixes. But let's be clear: repentance is not just another version of the marketplace's obsession with becoming fully self-actualized. *Our therapy culture says that you're a pretty good Joe or Jane, but you can be a better you. The Biblical call to repentance insists that you have sinned.* True repentance flows from the agonizing recognition that we have damaged and defiled ourselves and our world. *Real repentance painfully—sometimes tearfully—acknowledges that we have hurt people. We are not pretty good Joes and Janes.* Biblical repentance is not about becoming a better you; it's about becoming a different you—a new creation. Genuine repentance isn't about self-improvement; it's about transformation.

Some ancient traditions place this prayer on David's lips after his sin with Bathsheba, but nothing in the prayer specifically mentions David's sins of adultery and murder. Instead, this prayer was probably penned by some anonymous believer who craved purity of heart. *The psalmist contrasts human sin, iniquity, transgressions, and evil with God's loving kindness and tender mercies.* The God that the psalmist calls upon is not a self-help guru or "life-coach." Humans need more than a friend with a helping hand. God isn't just a better version of what we are. God's goodness is different from ours in kind, not just in degree. True repentance recognizes the impassable gulf between our inherent unrighteousness and God's inherent righteousness. *Human beings don't need to be improved, updated, or revised like a new edition of our favorite book or computer program; we need to be washed, purged, recreated, remade and restored. We are broken in a way that no quick fix can repair.*

Some people are perfectly willing to rebuke the sins of world, but are reluctant to address their own sin in anything other than the most abstract terms. This psalmist did the exact opposite. The psalmist practiced intense repentance in the first person (the words "I," "me," and "my" appear 35 times in this prayer). Yet the psalm offered only one comment about the sins of others (*"**Then** I will teach transgressors"*). I once heard a preacher say that *it takes less righteousness to criticize than to do anything else on earth. I think the psalmist would agree.* The psalmist wouldn't even mention other people's sins without first cataloguing the psalmist's own sins *ad nauseam.* If fully acknowledging our own sins is the first prerequisite for addressing the sins of others (and it is!), then the second qualification is the psalmist's broken, contrite, and worshipping heart. It may sound trite, but it's true—apart from an ongoing spirit of repentance, worship is a sham. When offered in a spirit of repentance, the forms of worship—what the psalmist called burnt offerings and whole burnt offerings—are flexible.

What have I learned from praying this prayer? Perhaps just this... *nothing makes me more generous in dealing with others— others' sins and others' worship—than a good, hard look into my own unrighteousness.*

Lord, be merciful to me, a sinner.

Jonah's Prayer from the Deep Sea

*"I called out of my distress to the LORD, and He answered me.
I cried for help from the depth of Sheol; You heard my voice.
"For You had cast me into the deep, into the heart of the seas,
And the current engulfed me.
All Your breakers and billows passed over me.
"So I said, 'I have been expelled from Your sight. Nevertheless I will
look again toward Your holy temple.'
"Water encompassed me to the point of death.
The great deep engulfed me,
weeds were wrapped around my head.
"I descended to the roots of the mountains.
The earth with its bars was around me forever,
But You have brought up my life from the pit, O LORD my God.
"While I was fainting away, I remembered the LORD,
And my prayer came to You, into Your holy temple.
"Those who regard vain idols forsake their faithfulness,
But I will sacrifice to You with the voice of thanksgiving.
That which I have vowed I will pay.
Salvation is from the LORD."
Jonah 2 (New American Standard Bible)*

People pray in all kinds of places—in planes, trains and automobiles; in churches, chapels and cathedrals; in classes, at baseball games and over dinner table. But of all the places that people have ever prayed, the location of this prayer has to be the strangest. Submariners have undoubtedly offered their fair share of prayers from the deep, but Jonah's deep sea submersible was like no other. Jonah was in the belly of a great fish—and apparently tangled up in sea weed.

Jonah's story is well-known. God told Jonah to go to Nineveh, but Jonah more or less told God to go jump in the lake. Jonah chartered a voyage to Tarshish, God sent a storm, the ship's crew grew scared, Jonah got pitched overboard, a fish took the bait, God finally had Jonah's undivided attention, and we get to overhear this prayer. Most of the prayer recounts Jonah's scrape with death—wind, waves, water, seaweeds, immense fatigue. Toward the end of the prayer, however, Jonah switched from the past tense ("I did" this and that) to the future tense ("I will sacrifice...").

A couple of things have always fascinated me about this prayer. First, *Jonah was very honest about this unenviable situation (in the belly of a stinking fish) and about the cause for his situation.* It's tough to imagine anyone experiencing any desire to hang out with Jonah in the conditions that he describes in the first two thirds of this prayer. He's gripped by fear and threatened by death. And how did Jonah get in this mess? Jonah had refused to preach to those who worship vain idols, so God had placed Jonah in this aquatic custody—and only God could release Jonah from his subsurface detention.

Second, *Jonah was honest about his continued lack of enthusiasm for the calling that God had given him.* Given the limited options at hand, Jonah acquiesced to God's will and promised to voice his sacrifice of thanksgiving for God. After all, Jonah reasoned, salvation—for the people of Nineveh or anyone else—comes from God. So, just as he had previously vowed, Jonah went to Nineveh and preached. But Jonah was clear (it was a *sacrifice* of thanksgiving), his heart wasn't in it. When he arrived in Nineveh, he delivered the briefest sermon ever recorded: "Forty days and you will be destroyed" (just five words in Hebrew). Despite Jonah's lackluster homily, the people of Nineveh repented and God forgave them. Jonah had hoped to see the folks of Nineveh suffer, so their repentance and God's willingness to forgive them disappointed and angered him. Poor Jonah, his anger earned him a hefty tongue lashing from God as the conclusion to his story.

Jonah's prayer and his life story in Scripture has affected people in very different ways. On the one hand, Jonah's prayer has served as a model of honest confession. Sometimes we, like Jonah, stand under God's judgment for our unwillingness to obey God.

When this happens, I think that we should follow Jonah's example and be honest about both our disobedience and about God's judgment. *If we can't be honest about being placed under God's judgment, we'll probably never be able to honest about our need for God's deliverance from that judgment.* Self-deception is not a Christian virtue. Sometimes God places us under judgment for our own good, but we can't experience the intended good unless we first acknowledge the reality of judgment. On the other hand, Jonah's prayer has taught me that *sometimes obedience is a sacrifice.* Hopefully, we'll perform those sacrifices more gracefully than Jonah did, but *there's no reason to pretend that obedience is always easy. Salvation comes from God and God has the right to demand sacrifices from God's people.*

Lord, instill an urgency for your salvation within me.

The Pharisee & Tax Collector

God, I thank you that I am not like the rest of humanity—robbers, evildoers, adulterers—or even like this tax collector. I fast twice a week and give a tenth of all I get.
Luke 18:11-12

God, have mercy on me, a sinner.
Luke 18:13

Both the first prayer, offered by a Pharisee, and the second prayer, offered by a tax collector, are very familiar. Nearly everyone recognizes both prayers as part of Jesus' teaching about proper and improper attitudes. Most of us quickly dismiss the first prayer as arrogant and self-righteous, while we just as quickly embrace the second prayer. Few of us would even consider offering a prayer like the Pharisee's. Yet, *the Pharisee's prayer was probably true* (most Pharisees didn't commit theft or adultery, but did fast and tithe), *probably sincere* (most Pharisees didn't see themselves as they saw other people), *and completely wrongheaded.* The Pharisee did not understand to whom he was speaking.

When I was in college, one of my favorite professors once asked me to close my eyes and to imagine the following scene: It was judgment day and God was separating people to the right and the left. God looked at me and said, "Well done, you good and faithful servant." God had been pleased with my life and service. Eventually, when God finished separating the people, God said to those of us on the right, "Enter into the joys of your Lord." Then, a moment later, God looked at the people on the left and said, "Ah, what the heck, you come on in too." When my prof said that, my mouth dropped open and I thought, "they don't deserve it!" Then, in a calm and non-judgmental voice, the professor said, "If your first thought was 'they don't deserve it,' you still don't understand grace." The professor left the room without saying anything more.

31

The difference between the prayers of the Pharisee and the tax collector was not their truthfulness (both prayers were probably true), or their sincerity (both prayers were probably sincere). The difference between the prayers was their sense of need. *The Pharisee didn't need God; the tax collector was absolutely dependent upon God.* In our culture, one of the foremost virtues and one of the most important accomplishments is self-sufficiency. "Work hard and make a living for yourself." "Save money and create a comfortable retirement." "Establish a nest egg and be ready for a rainy day." Such slogans may make sense in the financial world, but things are different in the kingdom of God.

Grace alone ensures success in the heavenly economy. John Wesley understood this principle. Wesley began reading the New Testament in Greek while in the second grade, established a "holy club" while in college, experienced a "strangely warmed" heart while in adolescence, and committed the whole of his life to spreading holiness throughout the land. Yet, when the eighty-eight year old saint came down to die, he prayed only sentence, "Chief of sinners I am, but Christ died for me." Wesley realized that he did not "deserve it."

I do not know when I will die, but *I do know two things.* When I face judgment, *I will throw myself on the mercy of the court.* I do not now have—nor will I ever have—anything to offer God in my own defense. And, between this present day and that future day of judgment, *I will worship the God of all mercy.*

Lord, teach me to plead for, and revel in, the mercy of God.

The Repentance of the Remnant

'O my God, I am too ashamed and embarrassed to lift my face to you, my God, for our iniquities have risen higher than our heads, and our guilt has mounted up to the heavens. From the days of our ancestors to this day we have been deep in guilt, and for our iniquities we, our kings, and our priests have been handed over to the kings of the lands, to the sword, to captivity, to plundering, and to utter shame, as is now the case. But now for a brief moment favour has been shown by the LORD our God, who has left us a remnant, and given us a stake in his holy place, in order that he may brighten our eyes and grant us a little sustenance in our slavery. For we are slaves; yet our God has not forsaken us in our slavery, but has extended to us his steadfast love before the kings of Persia, to give us new life to set up the house of our God, to repair its ruins, and to give us a wall in Judea and Jerusalem.

'And now, our God, what shall we say after this? For we have forsaken your commandments, which you commanded by your servants the prophets, saying, "The land that you are entering to possess is a land unclean with the pollutions of the peoples of the lands, with their abominations. They have filled it from end to end with their uncleanness. Therefore do not give your daughters to their sons, neither take their daughters for your sons, and never seek their peace or prosperity, so that you may be strong and eat the good of the land and leave it for an inheritance to your children for ever." After all that has come upon us for our evil deeds and for our great guilt, seeing that you, our God, have punished us less than our iniquities deserved and have given us such a remnant as this, shall we break your commandments again and intermarry with the peoples who practise these abominations? Would you not be angry with us until you destroy us without remnant or survivor?

O LORD, God of Israel, you are just, but we have escaped as a
remnant, as is now the case. Here we are before you in our guilt,
though no one can face you because of this.'
Ezra 9:6-15 (New Revised Standard Version)

This is one of Scripture's most candid, but least well known, prayers of repentance. I suspect that this prayer isn't better known and more widely discussed for a couple of reasons. First, *the prayer is a real downer.* It not only talks about failure, it talks about repeated and unrelenting failure. It's frank. Israel has disregarded God's will; their deeds are evil and their guilt great. Ezra doesn't sugarcoat it. Israel had been judged before and that's why only a remnant of the Israelites was still around in Ezra's time. The shallow repentance of Israel's past hadn't changed the people a bit. Israel had a record of failure after failure and rebellion after rebellion.

There's something to be learned from Ezra's account of Israel's repeated failures and sins. In our culture, it's popular to deny being perfect and it's almost sheik to publicly acknowledge that we have made some unspecified mistakes. But we should never confuse such vague apologies and such abstract confessions with genuine repentance. *Genuine repentance is more than a simple acknowledge-ment of our undefined failures.* It is the sincere expression of our godly sorrow for having done what we know that we should not have done. True repentance, like that in Ezra's prayer, identifies exactly what we have done wrong and why it was wrong. When we sincerely repent—an act more appropriately done in private than in public—we should be precise in identifying the evil which we have committed. When is the last time that you named one of your specific acts or deeds as evil in God's eyes?

Second, *the prayer is less known not only because it's a downer, but also because it's hard on Israel's love, romance and hospitality toward their neighbors.* Ezra names the Israelites' marriages, and even their friendships, with the people around them as sinful. Not many of us are eager to label friendship, even friendship with unbelievers, as sinful. Most of us find it hard to understand how simply befriending the people around us could be sinful. What's going on here?

When Israel's story began in Genesis, God promised to bless all peoples of the earth through Abraham and Sarah. But, as Ezra's prayer explains, the Israelites had never remained faithful to God. Every time the Israelites became associated with the people around them, Israel gave up its own identity and became just like everyone else. Ironically, when the Israelites became like the people around them, they had nothing unique or important to give to those people. Because of Israel's repeated assimilation to the ways of its pagan neighbors, God's prophets and priests were forced to command the Israelites to separate themselves from the world.

I sometimes wonder how things would have gone if God could have trusted the Israelites to live righteously and to witness faithfully in midst of an unbelieving world. *How different would the world be if God had not been forced to separate the Israelites from the very people they were supposed to bless?* I don't know, but I do know this. I pray that God will make me trustworthy to play my role in the plans of God. I would not want my attraction to sin or my inability to withstand temptation to rob the people around me of the blessings of God. I want to be a trustworthy conduit of God's blessings. I also think that the pathway to such trustworthiness leads straight through the valley of sincere repentance.

Lord, save me from every sin that would damage others.

Prayers for Guidance & Direction

The prayers recited under this category are taken from the Old Testament, the New Testament and an unknown soldier. The two Biblical prayers are seeking God's guidance for the people of Israel and for the Church. I haven't heard either of these prayers used very often in worship. I've never heard the third prayer used in worship—perhaps because it doesn't come from the Bible. However, this third prayer is also about divine guidance, but in the form of retrospection on God's often unseen guidance.

Elijah's Prayer

At the time of sacrifice, the prophet Elijah stepped forward and prayed: "O LORD, God of Abraham, Isaac and Israel, let it be known today that you are God in Israel and that I am your servant and have done all these things at your command. Answer me, O LORD, answer me, so these people will know that you, O LORD, are God, and that you are turning their hearts back again."

1 Kings 18:36-37 (New International Version)
"This kind can only come out by prayer."
Mark 9:30

    Sometimes I feel like I'm the slowest learner on the planet. Over the years, I've often scurried off to tell a friend or a mentor about my "new" insight only to learn how truly "old" my insight really was. I can be really thick. The history of my "new" insights into Elijah's prayer provides a pretty good survey of my hard-headedness.

    I remember when I first heard this prayer and the accompanying story of Elijah's competition with the "prophets" of the Baal. I imagined how cool it would be to face down a bunch of false prophets—to make fun of them and to have God answer my prayer with a blaze of glory in the way that God answered Elijah. In my boyhood fantasies, I could almost imagine myself winning an Olympic gold medal in the international prayer competition. A deep-voiced announcer would explain my humble Christian origins as I stood on a raised platform with the band playing my favorite hymn. The Christian flag would be raised over my head while photographers flashed pictures of my pious smile. The cover of *Prayers Illustrated* would announce: "Phillips shatters world record for effectiveness in prayer." Maybe I would even get my picture on a box of communion wafers.

Of course, it wasn't long before I came to see that *God isn't some cosmic Santa Claus or sanctified genie*. God doesn't consult a naughty and nice list to figure who gets their prayers answered and who gets a lump of coal. And God's certainly not obliged to give us three wishes when we rub some magic bottle. But to be honest, for quite a while, I did treat prayer like a game of chance or an exercise in serendipity. *Although I never really said so, I acted as if prayer was a wager.* The cost was low and pay-off was potentially high, so why not give prayer a shot? I took chances on prayer like some people take chances on slot machine or lottery tickets. It never hurts to try—maybe I'll get lucky.

At some point—I think that I got this "new" insight while I was in college—I began to understand that *prayer is not about bringing God into my service, prayer is about being drawn into God's service. Prayer isn't about "winning" or "getting lucky." It's about service.* Or, put more in even more basic terms, prayer isn't about self-indulgence. It's about self-sacrifice. After all, *God is not my servant; I am God's servant.*

We'll only see dramatic answers to prayer like Elijah saw when we come to see prayer as Elijah did. To be sure, God answered Elijah's prayer with a pretty spectacular display—hard to beat fire from heaven. But the desire behind Elijah's prayer wasn't to put on a show or even to win an individual competition. *Elijah wanted to bring the hearts of God's people back to their Lord.* For Elijah, prayer was an extension of his prophetic calling. *Elijah spoke the words of this prayer in order to direct the people of God back to their God.* The spectacular display of fire was merely an incidental means to that redemptive end.

How can we learn to pray as Elijah did—to pray in a way that transcends selfishness, personal ambition, and the need for recognition? How can we learn to pray for the benefit of all God's people? Ironically, if we want to learn how to pray well, we must pray often. Because, as Jesus said, this kind comes only through prayer.

Lord, school me in the ways of prayer.

38

Apostolic Decision-Making

*So two men stood up: Joseph called Barsabbas (also known as Justus)
and Matthias. Then they offered a prayer, "Lord, you know
everyone's heart. Show us which of these two you have chosen to
accept this ministry and apostleship, which Judas left to go where he
belongs."
Then they cast lots, and the lot fell to Matthias; so he was added to
the eleven apostles.
Acts 1:23-26*

Most of us want to do God's will. We love God. So, we want
to please God. We also believe that doing God's will is the surest
route to happiness. God understands the issues better than we do
and God loves us perfectly. So, why not trust God? And why not do
God's will. God's way is the best way.

Still, many Christians struggle over knowing the will of God.
For most of us, it's already been decided. *We're willing—maybe
even eager—to accept and follow God's will, but we're not always
clear on exactly what that will is.* That's certainly how the disciples
felt when they prayed this prayer. Jesus chose twelve disciples.
These twelve were to establish the New Testament people of God
just as Israel's twelve sons established the Old Testament people of
God. However, Judas betrayed Jesus and then took his own life. The
church was left with only eleven apostles. A twelfth apostle was
needed.

The apostolic selection process consisted of three stages.
First, the eleven apostles sorted through the 120 or so believers to
find people with two qualifications: long term experience with Jesus
(walked and talked with Jesus since his baptism) and direct
knowledge of the resurrection (have seen the resurrected Jesus in
person). The newest apostle would have to reliably communicate
Jesus' teachings and persuasively witness to his resurrection.
Second, the eleven apostles prayed over the two qualified

candidates.   Finally, the eleven apostles cast lots and selected Matthias.

To some, these elimination rounds may sound like an episode of "Apostolic Survivor: Jerusalem" or an ecclesiastical version of rock-paper-scissors (120, then 2, then 1). But the story is really about discerning God's will. The eleven apostles narrowed the options on the bases of their Christian convictions about Jesus. Then, they prayed and cast lots.

Lots were essentially dice with red and blue dots. Two blues meant "yes;" two reds meant "no." One of each color meant throwing the dice again. Casting lots was common in the OT, but it wasn't a distinctively religious method of decision-making. The soldiers who crucified Jesus cast lots to determine the new owners of Jesus' clothes (Luke 23:34). *So, what are we to make of casting lots?*

When I was in seminary, one of my friends was offered the opportunity to pastor two different churches. Both churches, both church boards, and both district superintendents had prayed over these offers and had decided that it was God's will for this young person to pastor each of their churches. The churches were in different states and hundreds of miles apart. My friend obviously couldn't pastor both churches, so she went to one of the professors for advice. *The professor simply said, "Do whatever you want. Both options sound good to me."*

Maybe that's how casting lots works. *Either candidate would make a great apostle and either one could serve the church well and fulfill God's will for the church.* I suspect that this is often the case. If we have diligently worked to discern what is not God's will (eliminated all but two of the 120) and sincerely prayed and remained open to God's leading, then God grants us the freedom to make our decision. *If both heads and tails would be within God's will, then it's probably okay to flip a coin.*

This apostolic casting of lots has helped me to understand that God's will is usually boarder and more inclusive than we think. Of course, God sometimes speaks very directly to us and we should always be open to that guidance, but God has also given us the freedom to make many choices for ourselves. *Prayer helps to choose from among the many good choices that remain after all the wrong choices have been eliminated* (it's not like Joseph/Barsabbas/Justus suddenly became evil just because he wasn't chosen). When seeking God's will , we should consider the apostolic approach: *eliminate what cannot be God's will, pray and remain open to God's further direction, make the decision in a peaceful manner, then be content that we have chosen one good option from among the many good options that God has provided.*

Lord, help me to avoid the wrong and to seek the good.

The Soldier's Prayer

I asked God for strength, that I might achieve,
I was made weak, that I might learn humbly to obey.
I asked for health, that I might do great things,
I was given infirmity, that I might do better things.
I asked for riches, that I might be happy.
I was given poverty, that I might be wise.
I asked for power, that I might have the praise of men,
I was given weakness, that I might feel the need of God.
I asked for all things, that I might enjoy life.
I was given life, that I might enjoy all things.
I got nothing that I asked for—but everything I had hoped for.
Almost despite myself, my unspoken prayers were answered.
I am, among all men, most richly blessed.

As with many classic prayers, we are uncertain who wrote this prayer. Some traditions attribute the prayer to a soldier who suffered a permanent disability in the American Civil War. The content and tone of the prayer certainly are consistent with that origin, but we can't be sure. Regardless of the prayer's origin, its insights into both Christian life and the nature of divine gifts are profound.

The prayer is *a testimony about the unintended consequences of prayer.* Throughout the passing seasons of this anonymous author's life, he or she made what seemed like legitimate and innocent requests for the resources—strength, health, riches, and power—that could fuel a life of service and accomplishment. These requests were not wrong in themselves; they contained nothing blatantly selfish or evil. In fact, God needs people with stamina, vigor, financial resources and personal influence. Such things are required. *The author's original requests were not crass or sinful, but they were naïve and unwise.*

42

Even our most sincere prayers for divine guidance can be easily co-opted by our undisciplined desires. It's natural for humans—particularly those with righteous enthusiasm for Christ—to want to accomplish great things for God. Our culture can subtly condition us to steer our deep love for God in the direction of personal achievement. If we carelessly presume the purity of our motives, we face the peril of forgetting that *we don't often have the wisdom to ask for the things that we truly need from God.* Too often, *we devise our own grandiose plans—only thinly disguising our own ambitions—and then ask God to bless those plans.* We must remain forever vigilant, lest our motives become tainted. Our desires for significance and recognition are relentless and insidious in their stealthy persistence.

This prayer's author came to recognize the audacity of prescribing our needs to God. *God knows what we need. Even more importantly, God knows what God needs.* Who isn't willing to be a dashing success for God? But what if Christ needs a noble failure? The blessings of elapsed time had taught this prayer warrior that the heavenly hosts have never had to exhaust themselves searching for people who were willing to accept privilege and prestige in the name of Christ. The Kingdom never suffers from a lack of people who are willing to serve a God who stands at their beck and call, quickly and abundantly provisioning their every perceived need.

The quiet and peaceful spirit who penned these words had learned that it is probably unwise—and certainly naïve—to presume that we know what God should give us to do God's will. *We humans are so prone to forget our proper place.* It is God who made us and not we ourselves. It is not ours to prescribe our role and stature in God's Kingdom. We are foolish to fix our hearts on privilege, position or even opportunity. Rather, our hearts should cry out for character, virtue and Christlikeness. When we have been schooled in the ways of humility, obedience, wisdom, and the desire for God, then we will be ready for whatever service comes our way. *What we need most is often what we desire least.* Let us pray that God will be kind enough to give us what we need and not merely what we ask for.

When we pray for guidance, we should remember the counsel derived from this prayer. *Our ambitions can only be fulfilled after they have been transformed.*

Lord, give me what only you know I need.

Prayers of Intercession

All five of the prayers recited under this category are taken from the Bible—one from the Old Testament and four from the New Testament. One of the prayers is attributed to Moses, one to Paul, and three to Jesus. Each of Jesus' prayers is quite familiar to Christians through their use in worship. The Pauline prayers are also familiar to many people, although the Mosaic prayer is probably not as well known. Each prayer is seeking God's blessing upon someone other than the person who was saying the prayer. When people say "I'll pray for you," they are referring to this kind of intercessory prayer.

Paul's Prayers for the Churches

*And I pray this: that **your love may increase** more and more in knowledge and depth of insight, so that you may be able to discern what is best and may **be pure and blameless** until the day of Christ, filled with the fruit of righteousness through Jesus Christ to the glory and praise of God.*
Philippians 1:9-11

*Now may our God and Father himself and our Lord Jesus clear our way to come to you. May the Lord make your **love increase and overflow** for each other and for everyone else, just like ours does for you. May the Lord strengthen your hearts so that you will be **blameless and holy** in the presence of our God and Father when our Lord Jesus comes with all his saints.*
1 Thessalonians 3:11-13

*May the very God of peace, **make you holy** through and through. May your whole spirit, soul and body be kept **blameless** at the coming of our Lord Jesus Christ. The one who calls you is faithful and will do it.*
1 Thessalonians 5:23-24

I know hundreds, maybe thousands, of ministers. At every stage of my adult life, I've been surrounded by clergy. All through college, seminary, and graduate school, I studied with future pastors and we learned from former pastors. As a professor, I've taught among all manner of clergy—from small town Baptists to uptown Methodists. Whether holiness preachers or celibate bishops, I count them all as friends and colleagues. I sometimes suspect my speed dial and my address book could serve as a primer for composing a *Who's Who among the Ordained and Soon-to-be Ordained.* I am truly blessed and I wish that everyone could know these divinely called men and women who are my friends.

The Apostle Paul, the author of the prayers quoted here, was a missionary. In fact, Paul was the first missionary. Paul routinely preached in places where no one else had ever spoken the name of Christ. Paul was an evangelist to the uninitiated. His ministry to the people who first read these prayers in Thessalonica and Philippi was tough. These people were serving pagan gods when Paul arrived in town. They hadn't even heard of the Old Testament, let alone of the Christ who fulfilled the OT. In these prayers—the first words from Paul since he had left that part of northern Greece—Paul tried to communicate his heart's deepest longings for these new believers.

Paul had a great many desires for these new believers. Of course, the bonds that they shared at the level of friendship made Paul desire a personal, face-to-face visit with them. And because of his deep pastoral sensitivities, Paul wanted the Philippians and Thessalonians to develop knowledge, insight and discernment. Paul likewise prayed for their strength of heart. All of these petitions were important to Paul, but they were all simply a means to an end. *The ultimate goal—the one recurrent aim of each of these prayers— was that these people would be found holy, pure, and blameless at the time of Christ's return.* Of course, Paul fully understood that no amount of personal determination or individual fortitude could enable these fresh converts to withstand the assaults of their pagan world. So, Paul assured them that God is faithful and he prayed that God would make them holy!

We can think about this prayer from two very different perspectives. From the perspective of Paul, the minister and the people's advocate in prayer, the prayer shows Paul's respect for the patience of God. Paul took the long view—he didn't pray for immediate gratification. Minor missteps would no doubt occur, but Paul understood that holiness—while attainable in this life—often develops slowly. And so, Paul prayed for his congregations to finish well. Paul had no exaggerated short term expectations for these new converts, he was confident that God could make them holy and fully loving—even blameless.

From the perspective of Philippians and Thessalonians, the prayer reveals their pastor's dreams for them. Paul knew that Christ would someday return for his people—and Paul was praying with that day in mind. Paul didn't pray that these folks would learn to obey him or would suddenly fall in step with his leadership. Instead, Paul prayed that they would love one another, that they would be holy and that they would be found blameless at Christ's return. If I could give one piece of advice to the church, it would be this: *read these prayers and understand, this prayer expresses how your pastor feels about you.* Your pastor rejoices in what God's grace can accomplish in your life—and *your pastor's heart throbs with prayers in your behalf.* That's what I've learned from reading Paul's prayers and from hanging around so many preachers over the years.

Lord, teach me to intercede for your people.

Moses' Prayer of Desperation

Then the LORD said to Moses, "Go down, because **your people, whom you brought up out of Egypt,** have become corrupt. They have been quick to turn away from what I commanded them and have made themselves an idol cast in the shape of a calf. They have bowed down to it and sacrificed to it and have said, 'These are your gods, O Israel, who brought you up out of Egypt.'
"I have seen these people," the LORD said to Moses, "and they are a stiff-necked people. Now leave me alone so that my anger may burn against them and that **I may destroy them. Then I will make you into a great nation."**
But Moses sought the favor of the LORD his God. "O LORD," he said, "why should your anger burn against your people, whom **you brought out of Egypt** with great power and a mighty hand? Why should the Egyptians say, 'It was with evil intent that he brought them out, to kill them in the mountains and to wipe them off the face of the earth'? Turn from your fierce anger; relent and do not bring disaster on your people. Remember your servants Abraham, Isaac and Israel, to whom you swore by your own self: 'I will make your descendants as numerous as the stars in the sky and I will give your descendants all this land I promised them, and it will be their inheritance forever.' " Then the LORD relented and did not bring on his people the disaster he had threatened.
Exodus 32:7-14 (English Standard Version)

I speak the truth in Christ. I am not lying. My conscience confirms me by the Holy Spirit. There is a great sorrow and unceasing anguish in my heart. For I could wish that I myself were cursed and cut off from Christ for the sake of my brothers and sisters, those of my own race, the people of Israel.
Romans 9:1-4

Intercession—praying for God's blessings upon another person—has almost become commonplace in our churches. We make, hear and respond to prayer requests in our fellowship circles, at our bible studies, and among our small groups. We hear that someone's child is ill, and we pray for the child. A newly married couple is experiencing difficulty in their relationship, and we promise to pray. A friend has lost a loved one, again we offer prayer. We've all prayed for our friends' broken bones and broken marriages, their wayward finances and their wayward children, even their lost pets and lost keys.

It is good that we pray for one another. Both *our intercession for others and their intercession for us are part of God's plan. It is our privilege and responsibility to bear one another's burdens*. The people of God are bound together by the adhesive power of mutual prayer. We seek healing for the sick and afflicted, justice for the persecuted and oppressed, and mercy for the guilty and graceless. We pray for another; we pray for all people.

Such prayers are altogether fitting and proper. However, I sometimes wonder if the sheer volume of our collected prayers can desensitize us to the seriousness of prayer. Can we allow prayer to become so pervasive that it becomes passionless—or even routine? Can our requests become so run-of-the-mill and casual that prayer becomes almost flippant? Can our many words and our much speaking numb us to the painful side of intercession? I fear that *if our prayers demand very little from us, then we may be tempted to treat prayer as if it has very little real value.*

These two prayers—one from Moses and one from the Apostle Paul—give us a different perspective on intercession. In the first prayer, Moses prayed for the Israelites and begged God to remain faithful to them—even after God had offered to establish a new people through Moses. Rather than jumping on God's offer of blessing for himself and his descendants, Moses begged God to return God's favor and blessing to the descendents of Abraham and Sarah. In the second prayer, the Apostle Paul was so distressed over the fate of Israel that he was willing to forfeit his own salvation for the sake of Israel. Both Moses and Paul prayed so earnestly for others that they lost all regard for their own well-being. Moses was willing to reject God's deepest blessings for himself and his descendants; Paul was willing to reject even salvation itself. *Such intercession transcends mere well-wishing.* It demands complete participation in the plight of those for whom we pray. These prayers express an unyielding and uncompromising—even a selfless—longing for the well-being of others.

Overhearing these prayers teaches us about the seriousness of prayer. *How nonchalant would we be about intercession if we were to follow the example of Moses and Paul?* What would our prayers sound like if we cried out for people so intently that we became willing to redirect God's blessings away from ourselves and toward others. While not all intercession will reach this intensity, the deepest recesses of intercession are probably found in this simple prayer: "Lord, give these people every blessing that you have intended for me." *Intercession is serious business; it's as serious as the cross that makes it possible.* Let us not make a farce out of bearing one another's burdens.

Lord, terrify me over the fate of the world.

Jesus' Prayer for Peter

"Simon, Simon, Look, Satan has asked to sift you as wheat. But I have prayed for you, Simon in order that your faith may not fail. And when you have turned back, strengthen your fellow believers."
Luke 22:31-32

We all have our "likes" and "dislikes." As for me, I don't like limits and I don't like waiting. I cringe at the sight of a "limit 3" sign in the grocery store and nothing irks me like those "quantities limited" footnotes in the fine print of an advertisement. Speed limit signs make me groan—and I can't even express the dismay brought on school zones. I always seem to be in a hurry (even when I have no real reason to hurry). And waiting? If I had written Dante's *Inferno*, the final stop would be a "waiting room."

We live in the age of instant gratification and immediate results. In most of our transactions, *we're used to getting what we want and getting it when we want it.* Science, technology, and a hypercompetitive marketplace have propelled our culture to previously unimagined efficiency and ease of delivery. Unfortunately, we sometimes get spoiled and begin to transfer the expectations of our consumer driven culture to the spiritual realm. If we aren't careful, we can develop what a friend of mine calls a "zap" theology. Ask God for something, and "zap," there it is—like hot tea from a replicator on the star ship Enterprise. For some people, true faith can slap a quick patch on any leak in the dike. *The equation is simple: prayer plus faith equals "zap."*

Of course, most of know that the Christian faith isn't about "quick and easy." Zap theology may sound good in theory, but it falls flat in the real world of our frustrated expectations, delayed dreams and revised plans. We remain hopeful—even expectant—but our gratification is often deferred rather than immediate. Our sovereign Lord works in a world of human freedom and frailty. Jesus' report about the anticipated outcome of his own prayer acknowledges just how our human condition can limit the effectiveness of prayer. *Jesus prayed that Peter would not fail, but Jesus acknowledged that Peter would still fail in spite of Jesus' prayer.* So, Jesus also prayed for Peter's renewed mission after he returned from his failure.

If there's ever been anyone who had true faith or anyone whose prayers could not fail, surely it was Jesus. Yet, Peter denied knowing Jesus even after Jesus had prayed that Peter's faith would not fail. *Peter denied knowing Jesus in spite of Jesus' prayers. Not even Jesus' prayers could keep Peter's faith from failing.* The effectiveness of even Jesus' prayers was limited by Peter's freedom to choose—and to choose badly.

When I become disappointed with the perceived ineffectiveness of my prayers for wayward loved ones, I think about this prayer. Even though Jesus knew that Peter's shortcomings would cause him to deny knowing Jesus, *Jesus did not grow disillusioned. Instead, Jesus prayed with a longer view in mind.* Jesus prayed for the stability of Peter's faith after he returned. Our prayers—like Jesus' prayers—are powerful, effective and transformative in the lives of those for whom we pray. Yet, the power of our prayers is limited by the freedom of human decision-making. "Zap" theology may be appealing, but it doesn't square with what we learn from Jesus' prayer. If we are to pray as Jesus prayed, we must learn patience. We must be willing to pray again when—in spite of our prayers—failure occurs.

If Jesus' prayers could fail to accomplish their objective, so can ours. *True faith may not produce instant results, but it does produce the patience to persist in prayer—even in the absence of instant results.*

Lord, give me the patience that does not come naturally.

Jesus' Final Prayer

"Father, forgive them, for they do not know what they are doing."
Luke 23:34

We store thousands, maybe millions, of images in our minds. When I think of prayer, my mind's eye sees images of pastors standing before congregations, of monks walking through a desert, of families sitting around the dinner table, of teens gathering around a flagpole, and of saints kneeling in cathedrals. The image here is very different. It's the image of a man hanging naked on a cross with blood oozing from his open wounds. A thief hangs on each side of this man as a few callous soldiers loiter beneath him, squabbling over the clothes that they have just ripped off him. I sometimes wonder if these soldiers paid any attention to the prayer that Jesus uttered in their behalf.

I've always believed in forgiveness. Over the years, I've asked for forgiveness, and been asked for forgiveness. I've been forgiven, and I have forgiven. But there's nothing in my experience that's comparable to this prayer. I've never asked God to forgive someone who was—at that very moment—humiliating me by parading my nakedness in public and murdering me through the slow tortures of crucifixion. What I know about forgiveness—and certainly any forgiveness that I have extended—is rendered completely trivial when compared to the full measure of forgiveness seen in this prayer. *A bloody, dying and naked Jesus, the very Son of God and the Savior of the world, was pleading with the Father of behalf of those who took amusement from his suffering.* The soldiers cast dice—played games and gambled, while Jesus' life drained away. Their disregard for the suffering just yards away from them is incomprehensible to me. How could they remain unmoved? I don't know. But to be honest, it's even more difficult for me to grasp how Christ could utter such a prayer. *How could any human being—even a human being who was also divine—be so forgiving?*

I suspect that this prayer haunts many of us. We know that we are supposed to forgive as Jesus forgave, but when we are wronged, we want to strike back at people or, at very least, we want to avoid any further interactions with the people who offend us. Of course, we all recognize that neither retaliation nor avoidance is consistent with Jesus' prayer. But still, for most of us, it isn't easy to move beyond the desire to get back at people. And even when we are able to control our impulse to get even, we're seldom eager to move beyond a polite disregard for those who have wronged us. Still, we read, "Father, forgive them."

For those of us who struggle with the words of this prayer, maybe the best advice is not to theorize about them, but rather to pray them. *This moment, think of some person, a specific person, who has wronged you.* Think about the person who has caused you the most pain, perhaps even a person who delights in making your life miserable. Think about a person who would smile if he or she heard that some hardship had come your way. *Now, pray for that person.* Pray that God will forgive that person—just as God has forgiven you. Pray that God will lavish divine love and blessing upon that person. Lift that person's name before God and ask God to prosper and protect that person. Plead with God to give that individual every good and perfect gift. Beg your Father to give that person peace that passes understanding and joy beyond measure.

At first, you may feel like a raging hypocrite as you offer this prayer. But if you stick with it, the grace of God will enable you to pray "Father, forgive them" and mean it.

Lord, bless my enemies.

Jesus' High Priestly Prayer

Father, the hour has come. Glorify your Son in order that your Son may glorify you. For you gave him authority over all people so that he might give eternal life to all those you have given him. This is eternal life: that they may know you, the only true God, and Jesus Christ, whom you have sent. I glorified you on earth by completing the work you gave me to do. And now, Father, glorify me before your presence with the glory I had with you before the world began.

*I have revealed you to those whom you gave me out of the world. They were yours; you gave them to me and they have obeyed your word. Now they know that everything you have given me comes from you. For I gave them the words you gave me and they received them. They truly knew that I came from you, and they believed that you sent me. **I pray for them. I am not praying for the world,** but for those you have given me, for they are yours. All I have is yours, and all you have is mine. And I am glorified through them. I will no longer remain in the world, but they are still in the world, and I am coming to you. Holy Father, protect them by the power of your name—the name you gave me—so that **they may be one as we are one.** When I was with them, I protected them and kept them safe by your name that you gave me. None has been lost except the one doomed to destruction so that Scripture would be fulfilled. Now, I am coming to you, but I say these things while I am still in the world, so that they may have the full measure of my joy in them. I have given them your word and the world has hated them, for **they do not belong to the world any more than I belong to the world.** I do not pray for you to take them out of the world but for you protect them from evil. They do not belong to the world, even as I do not belong to it. Sanctify them by truth; your word is truth. As you sent me into the world, I have sent them into the world. I sanctify myself for them so that they too may be sanctified in truth. I do not pray for them alone. **I pray also for those who will believe in me through their message,** that **all of them may be one,** Father, just as you are in me and I am in you.*

*May they also be in us **so that the world may believe that you have
sent me**. I have given them the glory that you gave me so that **they
may be one as we are one**: I in them and you in me. **May they be
perfect in unity** to let the world know that you sent me and have
loved them even as you have loved me. Father, I want those you have
given me to be with me where I am, and to see my glory, the glory
you have given me because you loved me before the creation of the
world. Righteous Father, though the world does not know you, I
know you, and they know that you have sent me. I have made you
known to them, and will continue to make you known in order that
the love you have for me may be in them and that I myself may be in
them.*
John 17

People use their "alone time" differently. People listen to
music, read books, work crossword puzzles, play video games, or just
sit and think quietly. *Jesus prayed... and he prayed for you.*

This prayer, Jesus' longest recorded prayer, was spoken
during the last "alone time" that Jesus ever had on earth. Just
moments after completing this prayer, Jesus was arrested, sent to a
brutal show trial, then publicly lashed and murdered. Of course,
Jesus knew what lay before him—and he understood that he
couldn't waste these last few moments alone with his Father.

*If you knew that you were about to offer your very last
private prayer, what would you say?* Would you pray for yourself?
Jesus didn't. Would you pray about the great political and
ideological debates of the day? Jesus didn't. Would you pray for the
good of the whole world? Jesus didn't. In fact, Jesus explicitly said
that he was not praying for the world! Instead, Jesus focused his
prayer upon a single group—his small and frightened band of
followers.

In some ways, Jesus' refusal to pray for the world seems
strange—like a bizarre twist on the familiar message of God's great
love for the world. Most of us have memorized John 3:16 and we
know that Christ came into the world to save the world, but Jesus

didn't pray for the world in this prayer. In fact, when we look at this prayer closely, even the way that Jesus prayed for his followers seems skewed. Jesus didn't pray that his followers would win the world or that they would witness with boldness and effectiveness. Jesus didn't even pray that the church would grow. As a matter of fact, apart from a single line about the world coming to know that Jesus was sent by God, this prayer demonstrates no evangelistic fervor. In short, *this prayer is remarkably uninterested in the lost world and the task of evangelism.* Why?

At this critical point in time, Jesus had to focus on the single issue upon which everything else rested—the unity of God's people. Jesus repeatedly emphasized the crucial need for the believers to be unified. Jesus understood that his life's work could fall into disrepute. His redemptive mission could flounder. His followers absolutely could not degenerate into a bickering mob. This was no time for petty squabbles. *Jesus was depending upon those who bore his name to show the world the true extent of divine love.* Jesus hadn't come to assemble a coterie of the worldly minded. Gossips, backbiters and perpetual malcontents have nothing to offer a lost world. Jesus prayed that his followers would exemplify another way of living—a way of grace, compassionate, and harmony.

Do you want to make God's dreams come true? If so, do this. Offer the world an alternative to the competitive, me-first, ego-centric, way of the world. *Fix your heart on becoming one with your fellow believers*—becoming as supporting and gracious to God's people as God and Christ are to another. Give the world a vision of a community transformed by the one whose name we bear. Love your brothers and sisters in Christ; love them without reservation or self-regard. Love them for no other reason than that it is the right thing to do.

When I speak like this, some people object: "But the church is called to serve the world." That is true, but Jesus prayed for us— you and me—to live this way. And when we do, we will not only serve the world, we will transform it. And *until we live this way, we are not prepared to serve the world.* When we Christians live out our

58

shared identity in Christ, the world will recognize the love that comes from the one whose name we bear.

Lord, make us one.

Prayers of Praise

All three of the prayers recited under this category are taken from the New Testament—from Luke's Gospel, John's Gospel and the Book of Revelation. The prayers are attributed to Mary (the mother of Jesus), Zechariah (the father of John the Baptist), Thomas (also known as "doubting Thomas"), and an assortment of heavenly hosts. Each of these prayers is quite familiar to Christians through their use in worship. Some of these prayers have been set to music and thus adapted for musical worship.

Praise to the Lamb

*You are **worthy**, our Lord and God,*
to receive glory and honor and power,
because you created all things,
and through your will they were created
and have their being....
*You are **worthy** to take the scroll*
and to open its seals,
*because you were **slain**...*
***Worthy** is the Lamb, who was **slain**,*
to receive power and wealth and wisdom and strength
and honor and glory and praise!
Revelation 4:11; 5:9, 12

I once read a famous preacher write about how useful a good idea can be. He talked about how well some ideas had served him over the years, but then he explained that some ideas were so profound that he couldn't use them at all. Instead, these ideas had used him. Then, he began to list what he called "the ideas that have used me."

If there is a single idea that has used me, it is this idea—worthy is the lamb who was slain. Revelation 4-5 are the neglected crown jewels of the Christian faith. Many Christians, including some pastors and preachers, shy away from Revelation because they are uneasy with the violent interpretations often given to the book. Such well-meaning neglect of Revelation is a tragedy. Revelation is easier to understand than most people realize.

Revelation is structured around two images—the lamb and the beast. The beast brings violence, death and destruction upon the world—and ultimately upon himself; the lamb is slain, but ultimately triumphs over sin, death and destruction. The real question for understanding the book of Revelation is simply this: *Which creature will you follow, the lamb or the beast?* The lamb brings life through self-sacrifice; the beast brings death through self-indulgence.

Revelation 4-5 reveal a place where Christ reigns. There, God sits on a throne encompassed by a green rainbow, symbolic of God's life-giving promises to all the inhabitants of the earth. There, God is surrounded by creatures who sing praise to God. Each creature has eyes all around so that it can fully see and understand its proper role in creation. There, the eagle-like creatures of the air, the lion-like carnivores, and the ox-like herbivores all join humanity in singing praises to our God and King. There, before the throne of God, all the people of God assemble together and sing: "You are worthy, our Lord and God!" The twenty-four elders, who lead in praise, represent all the people of God through the ages (twelve tribes of Israel plus twelve apostles).

Having gazed into this throne room where all creation sings praises to God, the Revelator longs to know who will bring this new world into being. The angel points the Revelator toward "the lion of the tribe of Judah" (Rev. 5:5). The Revelator's heart must have swelled as his eyes searched for this lion. Only a mighty sweeping power of God could convert our sin-cursed into such a place. Then, as the Revelator looked toward the throne to see the lion who would reveal God's power, the Revelator saw a lamb who looked as it had been slain (5:6). At that point, *the awesome truth became clear—the power of God is revealed by a slaughtered lamb, not by a raging lion.* As the Revelator gazed upon the lamb, he heard the heavenly hosts singing to the lamb, "worthy is the lamb who was slain." And all the praise that was formerly given to God is now also given to the Lamb—because the Lamb is God!

This idea has used me. The God revealed in Jesus Christ is a slaughtered lamb, not a raging lion. *Our God does not overcome evil by the dominance of a raging lion; our God overcomes evil by the sacrifice of a self-giving Lamb.* I pray that I may have the courage to follow the self-sacrificing way of the Lamb.

Lord, worthy is the lamb who was slain.

Magnificat & Benedictus

My being magnifies the Lord and my spirit rejoices on account of God my Savior, because God has looked upon the lowliness of this servant of God. For, from now on, all generations will bless me because of what your great power did for me. God's mercy is for those who fear the Lord from generation to generation. God did mighty deeds with the divine arms, God scattered the arrogant in the attitudes of their hearts. God brought the powerful down from thrones and lifted up the lowly. God filled the hungry with good things and sent the rich away empty. In order to recall mercy, God helped God's child, Israel. The Lord did so just as God spoke to our ancestors, to Abraham and to his descendents forever.
Luke 1:47-55

May the Lord God of Israel be praised because the Lord has visited us and has brought redemption for God's people. God has raised up a horn of salvation for us in the house of God's child David. This is just what was spoken through the mouths of God's holy prophets from ancient times. We have salvation from our enemies and from the hand of all those who hate us. God practiced mercy with our ancestors and God remembered God's holy covenant. God gave us an oath which God swore to our father Abraham. Fearlessly, God rescued us from the enemies' hand so that we might serve the Lord in piety and righteousness before the Lord all of our days. But you also, child, will be called a prophet of the Most High. You will prophesy before the Lord to make the way ready. You will prophesy to give the knowledge of salvation to God's people in the forgiveness of their sins because of the tender mercy of our God by which sunshine from on high will visit us. You will prophesy to those who are sitting in darkness and in the shadow of death in order to establish our feet in the way of peace.
Luke 1:68-79

The traditional names of these prayers, "Magnificat" and "Benedictus," come from the first word of each prayer in Latin. The titles date back to the middle ages when these prayers were commonly recited by Christian monks during morning and evening Vespers. If you were a monk about a thousand years ago, you would probably begin your day with the Magnificat and end your day with the Benedictus. No other biblical prayers have been chanted more often in worship than these two prayers.

The church's history of using these prayers together in worship is quite consistent with their pairing in Luke's Gospel. Mary, the mother of Jesus, prayed the Magnificat after she learned that she was to give birth to Jesus. Zechariah, the father of John the Baptist, prayed the Benedictus after his wife, Elizabeth, gave birth to John the Baptist. Such pairing of a female and a male voice is common in Luke's Gospel and emphasizes our need to hear God's word from both male and female voices.

Protestant Christians—like me—are often uncomfortable with Mary's prophecy that future generations will rise up to call her blessed. However, this biblical announcement should not be ignored. Mary was indeed blessed. She was the mother of our Lord. A refusal to acknowledge Mary's role in the drama of salvation is incongruent both with Scripture and with much of Christian tradition. As the Apostle Paul said, Jesus was born of a woman. And as the angel said in Luke's Gospel, Mary was highly favored. God chose to form the redeemer inside a woman's body. To minimize Mary's involvement in redemptive history is to denigrate the place of women in God's plan for salvation. The Messiah did not arrive as an adult, but rather as an unborn infant to be nurtured and sustained within woman's uterus.

Both Zechariah's prayer for John and Mary's prayer for Jesus exalt the God who delivers salvation. *Both prayers express much of their praise in the past tense even though neither John nor Jesus had yet done much of anything*. These prayers exude confidence in God. They display the courage to thank God for the redemption that has been promised and begun, but not completed. We sometimes think about praise only as an expression of gratitude for what God has accomplished. But these prayers encourage us to think about praise in more comprehensive terms. Perhaps we should also conceive of praise as an expression of our confidence in what God will accomplish. *True praise not only rejoices in God's past acts, but also celebrates over God's future acts.* In difficult and uncertain times—like Mary's pregnancy—*try practicing the art of anticipatory praise.*

If you could praise God for only one thing at this moment, what would it be? If you have something in mind, ask yourself whether that thing is an individual blessing for you or a corporate blessing for all of God's people. These prayers offer thanks for both individual and community blessings (note the prevalence of "me," "I" and "my" in Mary's Magnificat and the virtual absence of these words in Zechariah's Benedictus). Without an individual connection, praise can become detached and formulaic; it can lack a spirit of intimacy. Without a corporate dimension, praise can become emotive and self-absorbed; it can lack a spirit of grandeur. Sincere and mature praise extols both God's goodness in my individual life and God's broader redemption in entire Christian community. God is worthy of all praise.

Lord, I praise you for all the good that you shall do.

Thomas's Prayer

"My Lord and my God"
John 20:28

A lot of people talked to Jesus. Pharisees and Sadducees, bleeding women and demon-possessed men, the lame, the blind, the rich and the poor, soldiers, scribes and disciples, politicians, preachers and tax collectors, Jesus talked with all of these people... and more. In our churches we often talk about Jesus' words—what Jesus said—but I sometimes wonder if we should spend more time listening to what Jesus heard.

A lot of what Jesus heard was like a lot of what we hear. Jesus heard people comment on everyday matters like the best fishing techniques and the nutritional needs of large crowds. Jesus fielded complaints and accusations, he handled requests and petitions. Desperate words formed pleas for healing and deceitful words tried to trap him. Even gossip and rumors made their way to his ears. Boasts and confessions, truth and lies, sincere and insincere flattery, Jesus heard it all—and he heard a lot of things over and over.

Of all the words uttered by Jesus' admirers and detractors, by his friends and adversaries, these simple words—"my Lord and my God"—stand out as the most unique. Thomas, the disciple forever dubbed "doubting Thomas," was the only person to ever call Jesus "Lord and God." Peter was the only disciple who came close to the depth of Thomas's confession. He once called Jesus "the Messiah," but not even Peter called Jesus "God." If Peter hit a homerun when he called Jesus the Messiah, Thomas hit a game-winning grand slam when he proclaimed Jesus to be God. Thomas's proclamation is even more impressive when we remember that Peter proclaimed Jesus as the Messiah only after Jesus had interrogated him; Thomas proclaimed Jesus as God after Jesus had merely invited Thomas's touch.

"My Lord and my God!" Who dared speak such words? Thomas, doubting Thomas, that's who! The only person in all the gospels to profess Jesus as Lord and God was same person who had so openly expressed his doubts just a few days earlier.

People come into my office after a chapel service or between classes, and after sitting around for a few minutes, they suddenly confess that they have doubts. Often these people feel guilty, or even ashamed and embarrassed. In their frustration, they usually blurt out something like "I don't know what to do with these doubts!" Then I smile in as comforting a way as I can and say, "Well, you seem to be doing the right things so far." Then we play the opposite game. I give them a word and they give me the opposite. For example, I say "light;" they say "dark." I say "up;" they respond "down." I say "faith." They aren't sure what to say, so I say "disbelief." The opposite of faith is not doubt, it is disbelief. *Doubt is not the absence of faith. Rather faith is the prerequisite for doubt; only those who have faith can doubt.* Doubt is usually a sign of faith growing, not faith dying.

If you struggle with doubt, do what Thomas did. Be honest with your fellow disciples about your doubt, but remain in the community of the faithful (as Thomas did). If you do these things, Christ can be trusted and he will make himself real to you. And someday, perhaps someday soon, you will hear these words well up from deep within your soul, "My Lord and my God."

Lord, may I cling to you as my lord and my God.

Prayers for Strength

All four of the prayers recited under this category are taken from the Bible (three from the New Testament and one from the Old Testament). The prayers are attributed to an unnamed father, to Jesus, to the apostles, and to Nehemiah. These prayers aren't often familiar to Christians. They are seldom used in worship. Each calls for strength for a different purpose, for healing, for preaching, for building, and for the cross.

The Unbelieving Believer's Prayer

Immediately the boy's father cried out, "I believe; help my unbelief!"
Mark 9:24

Who should pray? Easy answer: "everyone should pray." When should we pray? Another easy answer: "any time... all the time." Because the answers to these questions are so obvious, I'm left wondering why I so often act like I don't know these facts. Here's how it often happens with me— *I'm reluctant to pray at the precise moments when I most need to pray.* When I pass through the valleys of doubt, temptation, and trial, I often feel myself being lured away from prayer. When my obedience is lax, my walk is inconsistent, or my faith is faltering—the very thought of prayer can intimidate me. *My will to pray seems weakest at the exact times when my need to pray is strongest.* I suspect that I am not alone.

Given what prayer is, I suppose that it's somewhat natural for us to feel uneasy approaching God with tainted commitment and unworthy motives. After all, we think—who am I, a child of hell, to approach the throne of God? *We know ourselves—our faithless, doubting, disobedient and forlorn selves—and we know God. How could we—in our condition—dare address our Creator?* Our innate impulses tell us to hide our discouraged, doubting, or even sinful selves from God. When we sense the Spirit's gentle tug to fellowship we should leap toward the God who craves our company. After all, our most primal memories remind us that our God forever stands ready to forgive the sinful, strengthen the weak and embolden the despairing, but our more recent despairs discourage us.

Feelings of discouragement are common and understandable in the wake of wavering faith, but they are also unwarranted and irrational. Our ability to enter God's presence is always a gift of grace and never a product of our own merit. So, why should we allow an awareness of our failures to hamper us from pursuing God's counsel? *If we had to earn the privilege of the divine presence, when could we ever hope to speak with our Father?* God's not like some NBA talent scout who comes around from time to time to check on the all stars. God has an open door policy; God's invitation to communion has no preconditions or expiration date. God is always available at our earliest convenience. God wants to speak with us. Prayer is an opportunity extended to us through God's infinite goodness—and through that alone.

We can be tempted to think that our unworthiness excuses us from prayer, but God's forgiving, redeeming, and purifying grace renders such excuses simply irrelevant. In fact, God's love ensures that God is eager to hear our heart's concerns. Still, we sometimes avoid prayer simply because of our shame over not having believed or acted as we should have. Failure and embarrassment can leave us with an almost impenetrable barrier to prayer. *What if we have a hard time forgiving ourselves, believing in ourselves, and starting over?* Maybe we should pray this prayer: "Lord, I believe. Help thou my unbelief" (KJV).

Such prayer is much more than reciting some self-help slogan or giving ourselves a pep talk. Prayer like this is an acknowledgement of our perpetually mixed emotions. We love God and we believe in God's grace. However, our faith and our faithfulness are seldom perfect. We are absolutely dependent upon God's grace; we need help from beyond ourselves. We are not like the little engine that kept muttering "I think I can; I think I can; I think I can." *We are people who say, "I cannot; I cannot; I cannot, but God's grace is sufficient for me."* By the grace of God, we can overcome—if we learn to call out to God when we stumble.

Lord, establish my life in your perfection.

Take this Cup

"Abba, Father," he said, "everything is possible for you.
Take this cup from me. But not what I will, but what you will."
Mark 14:36

One of the most striking moments from my first teaching assignment came as I talked to a university president. I—while still in my first semester of university teaching!—was regaling this fellow with a boatload of advice about how to run a college. After quietly listening to me for several minutes, he leaned back and said, "In my job, there's no shortage of good advice." I understood what he meant. I changed the subject to a more casual line of conversation.

We live in an advice-rich culture. Most of us have a large reserve of good—but only partially used—advice. Doctors tell us to eat our vegetables, floss our teeth and watch our weight (diet and exercise!). Safety experts warn us to fasten our seat belts, look both ways before crossing the road, and keep our tires properly inflated. Educators want us to turn off the TV and read; fire marshals urge us to change the batteries in our smoke detectors; even veterinarians warn about fleas, ticks and various other parasites. *My friend taught me an important lesson—not many people run around looking for more good advice.*

I think that there are times when I treat God's will—God's clear and unambiguous directives for my life—as it was just another piece of good advice. But deep down I know that God's will is much more than good advice. The Savior's will shouldn't be treated like the platitude of the day or some passing fad. When God's will becomes clear to me—as it was clear to Jesus when he agonized over this prayer—I should do it. *God's will, when clearly known, is not negotiable.* I am convinced of this and I both truly know and firmly believe that doing God's will leads to both my redemption and the redemption of the world. I also understand both that God has the right to demand sacrifices from me and that God rewards sacrifice—even an ultimate sacrifice like Jesus made—with the power of the resurrection.

When I hesitate to do God's will, it isn't a problem of cognition. Intellectually, I understand the wisdom of always doing God's will. It's a matter of defiance. I have a will of my own and my will is not always consistent with God's will. *Let me be honest. If God demanded from me what God demanded from Jesus, I would hesitate.* Would I pray three times a day if it meant the lions' den as it did for Daniel? Could I leave everything as the rich young ruler was asked to do? Would I give every last morsel of my food to Elijah as the widow was commanded to do? I don't think that I would ever outright refuse to do God's will, but I can imagine myself hesitating— or perhaps even seeking a compromise with God.

If you're like me and you're not always able to pray "not my will, but yours be done" like Jesus did, then I want to give you some advice. Begin small. *If your will clashes with God's will, try giving the Lord permission to change your will.* If you can't immediately and enthusiastically submit to God's will, pray this: "Lord, I don't know if I'm willing to do what you ask, but I am willing to allow you to make me willing."

In time, step by step, the grace of God will enable you to pray—honestly and without mental reservation—"not my will but yours be done, O Lord!"

Lord, give me a will to do your will.

Prayer for Boldness
in the Midst of Persecution

When released, Peter and John went back to their own people and reported what the chief priests and elders had said to them. Those who heard this report raised their voices together in prayer to God. "Sovereign Lord," they said, "you made the heaven and the earth and the sea, and everything in them. You spoke by the Holy Spirit through the mouth of your servant, our father David:
" 'Why do the nations rage and the peoples plot in vain? The kings of the earth take their stand and the rulers gather together against the Lord and against his Anointed One. For in truth, Herod and Pontius Pilate met together with the Gentiles and the people of Israel in this city to conspire against your holy servant Jesus, whom you anointed. They did what your hand and will had said beforehand was to happen. Now, Lord, consider their threats and enable your servants to speak your word with great boldness. Stretch out your hand to heal and perform miraculous signs and wonders through the name of your holy servant Jesus." After they prayed, the place where they were meeting was shaken. And they were all filled with the Holy Spirit and spoke the word of God with boldness.
Acts 4:23-31

I've never been in jail, prison, or any other kind of involuntary custody. I've never been publicly beaten, or even experienced any significant threat to my physical well-being. Of course, I've been frightened by this or that from time to time. I've even allowed myself to grow quite scared a few times. But, in retrospect, none of these perceived threats was very real. In fact, I never faced anything—other than the possibility of some unforeseen accident or illness—that could justify any deep-seated fear on my part. *My life has been pretty easy; I've enjoyed a cushy existence. Peter and John couldn't say that.* They faced clear and present danger—and they prayed about that danger.

73

When Peter and John offered this prayer, they had just been released from the custody of the Sanhedrin. That incarceration could easily have ended with their deaths. These same people had instigated Jesus' death just a few months earlier. The temple authorities weren't kidding with Peter and John; *Peter and John had received credible death threats.* The people who raged against the apostles weren't bluffing or making idle threats. When the apostles offered this prayer, they were confronting the same hostile forces which had nailed Jesus to the cross.

Given the threat they faced, it's hardly shocking that the apostles prayed. However, the content of their prayer is surprising. The apostles did not pray for their deliverance from danger or even removal of the threat. Instead, they asked God to consider or look at their situation and then give them courage to face it. *The apostles' extraordinary prayer asked God to give them boldness and courage commensurate with the threat before them.* Amazingly, they even asked God to equip them to perform signs and wonders. The apostles undoubtedly understood the significance of their request. Performing signs and wonders meant drawing more attention to themselves. The more attention they drew to themselves, the more likely they were to be persecuted and victimized. *The apostles were seeking the courage and capacity to be further persecuted for the cause of Christ.*

The gospel has come down to us at a very high price. One early Christian writer said that the blood of the martyrs is the seed of the church. Untold hosts of saints have sacrificed life and limb so that we may hear Christ's words. Stephen was stoned, and James was murdered with the sword. Paul was beheaded, and Peter was crucified. Christian leaders like Perpetua, Thecla and Ignatius were thrown to lions, torn limb from limb, and stomped by elephants. When the emperor Nero discovered Christians who refused to worship him, he ordered their tongues cut out and their teeth broken. In what one Roman historian called the utmost refinement of cruelty, Nero even smeared believers with hot tar and burned them alive before his terrified dinner guests.

This faith has come to us at a great price. I will not dishonor the sacrifices of the saints and martyrs of the past by comparing myself to them. However, I do pray that God will grant me the small parcel of courage needed to speak the gospel boldly in spite of whatever minor inconveniences and annoyances I may encounter for the cause of Christ.

Lord, may I live worthy of the sacrifices of the saints.

Strength to Build

They were all trying to frighten us, thinking,
"Their hands will get too weak for the work, and it will not be
completed."
But I prayed, "Now strengthen my hands."
Nehemiah 6:9

Why don't more people achieve great things for God? Why don't people accomplish more for Christ, for the church, for humankind, for the world? More than any other reason, it's because they don't try to accomplish more. It's not that they are incapable, or even unwilling. It's that they're inactive. People who don't accomplish much usually share one trait in common: they don't try to accomplish much. *The greatest obstacle to achieving great things is not the failure to succeed; it's the failure to try.* People accept the lie that they can't do what needs to be done. They see the need—sometimes even the potential—for change, but they don't believe they can pull it off. So, discouragement, complacency and inactivity win—and they do nothing.

When Nehemiah and his fellow believers finally got to Jerusalem after their exile in Babylon, they found Yahweh's temple in ruins. Their homes, barns and businesses were destroyed—burned to the ground. Livestock had been stolen or scattered. Their orchards had been hacked down and their fields were overgrown with weeds and scrub. Nothing looked right; nothing worked like it should. And to top it all off, the people in the surrounding area were hostile to Nehemiah's plans for rebuilding Jerusalem and God's temple. If Nehemiah and his colleagues were going to rebuild Jerusalem, they would have to do it with a hammer in one hand and a sword in the other. Times were tough, and the task was immense. Circumstances were overwhelming. Resources were thin, and resolve was weak. People everywhere were saying that this project wasn't going to be completed. *No doubt, many people were calling* on Nehemiah to be "realistic." Some things really are impossible. Conventional wisdom was asking "why try?"

What do you do when common sense leads you to conclude that the mission cannot be accomplished? When the need completely outweighs the available resources? When success is all but impossible, and even a limited success is unlikely? Why not pray Nehemiah's prayer? "Now, strengthen my hands."

God works through inadequate people—or at least through people with enough honesty and humility to have profound doubt about their own abilities. If you're plagued by self-doubt and personal uncertainty, don't sweat it. *God specializes in giving undaunted courage to those in daunting circumstances.* It's not about you. It's about God working through you—and God has supplied you with far more potential than you realize. It's simple—if God has called you to the task, God will be faithful. You can accomplish extraordinary things... if you try. God will strengthen you... if you ask.

Sadly, many believers surrender to outward appearance. They fail without a fight. The potential lies fallow for years, or even for a lifetime. Still, God stands ready, willing, and eager to strengthen them if they will merely ask. The economy of grace knows no shortage of unfulfilled potential or unused gifts. Lord, strengthen our hands to do your work. At very least, Lord, give us the courage to keep our hands to the work set before us.

Lord, give me much work to do and the faithfulness to complete it.

Prayers of the Unspeakable

All the prayers recited under this category are taken from the Old Testament (from the Psalms, from Isaiah, from Genesis, from Isaiah and from 1 Kings). Most of these prayers are not at all familiar to Christians. Nearly all of these prayers are notable for their almost complete absence from Christian worship. In fact, some Christians will be surprised to learn that some of these prayers are even in the Scriptures. Yet each of these prayers is significant in its own way.

Sarah's Laughter

*Then **the LORD said**, "**I will** surely return to you about this time next year, and Sarah your wife will have a son." Now Sarah was listening from tent's entrance behind Abraham. Abraham and Sarah were already old and well advanced in years. Sarah was past the age of childbearing. So Sarah laughed to herself as **she thought**, "After **I am** worn out and my husband is old, **will I** now have this pleasure?" Then the LORD said to Abraham, "**Why did Sarah laugh** and say, 'Will I really have a child, now that I am old?' **Is anything too hard for the LORD?** I will return to you at the appointed time next year and Sarah will have a son." Sarah was afraid, **so she lied** and said, "I did not laugh." But the Lord said, "Yes, you did laugh."*
Genesis 18:10-15

Sarah laughed at God and then she lied to cover it up. Most of us understand that fibbing to an all-knowing deity is a losing proposition (it's not like anyone actually gets away with it!). But *look at what Sarah and Abraham had been through.*

God promised to give Abraham and Sarah many descendents. Time passed—and the stork never visited. Abraham grew close to his nephew Lot, but Lot went his own selfish way. More time passed—and the nursery remained empty. Abraham grew close to another young man, Eliezer of Damascus. But the lad drifted away and the couple still had no heirs. Still more time passed—and the couple desperately longed for a child. Eventually Sarah offered Abraham a sexual surrogate. Sarah's servant, Hagar, had a son with Abraham. But Hagar's son, Ishmael, did not fulfill God's promise. God had promised that Abraham *and Sarah* would have a child together.

God had made a promise to Abraham and Sarah. *The couple had tried to fulfill that promise through ordinary means, but each scheme was unsuccessful.* Each heir apparent—the nephew, Lot; the Damascus kid, Eliezer; and even the half-son, Ishmael—failed to garner divine approval. The post-menopausal Sarah was now 90 years old and the less than virile Abraham was 99. No one expected to see Abraham and Sarah attending birthing classes. Then God spoke—and Sarah laughed.

Why wouldn't Sarah laugh? Who ever heard of someone becoming a mother at more than 90 years old? *Sarah was shocked.* She had long ago given up any hope of having a child of her own. So, when God announced that she was to have a child, she laughed. An over-the-hill couple like Abraham and Sarah could never accomplish such a thing.

On the one hand, *Sarah's ability to hear such improbable words is admirable.* If God said something this unbelievable to most of us, we would dismiss the divine voice without much serious consideration. Sarah's laughter—as impious as it seems at first glance—displays a truly remarkable willingness to hear God's voice. Too often, our ears are so attuned to the familiar that we cannot even hear when God says the unexpected. Our lowered expectations can squeeze the divine voice into muted and mundane tones—not so with Sarah. She could hear God speaking even in the most laughable ways.

I'm curious. *When's the last time that God shocked you?* When's the last time that God's clear promises and plans seemed too outlandish to be true? When's the last time that you were absolutely certain that you couldn't do what God was calling you to? If God hasn't shocked you in a while, pray for a divine vision that transcends the mediocre. God may have bigger dreams than you realize.

On the other hand, however, Sarah didn't hear God's voice very clearly. *God said, "I will." Sarah replied, "I can't" and "I'm not able to."* But all of Sarah's protests about her own supposed insufficiencies were rendered silly by a single divine question—"Is anything too difficult for God?" *When we find ourselves overwhelmed by God's promises, our most faithful response may be to laugh with Sarah.* The initial utterances of a sincere faith may be to say, "I can't even imagine doing that. It's laughable." But the next

80

utterances of that same faith may be to say, "Lord, if it's going to happen, you'll have to do it."

Divine love knows no impossibilities. God specializes in extreme measures—death to life and darkness to light. Such measures are routine to God. *Lord, let us not truncate your promises by looking to our own resources.*

Lord, entrust me with the absurdities of your love.

Prayers from Exile

Appoint someone evil to oppose my enemy;
let an accuser stand at his right hand.
When he is tried, let him be found guilty,
and may his prayers condemn him.
May his days be few; may another take his place of leadership.
May his children be fatherless and his wife a widow.
May his children be wandering beggars;
may they be driven from their ruined homes.
May a creditor seize all he has;
may strangers plunder the fruits of his labor.
May no one extend kindness to him
· or take pity on his fatherless children.
May his descendants be cut off,
their names blotted out from the next generation.
May the iniquity of his fathers be remembered before the LORD;
may the sin of his mother never be blotted out.
May their sins always remain before the LORD,
that he may blot out their name from the earth.
For he never thought of doing a kindness, but hounded to death the
poor
and the needy and the brokenhearted.
He loved to pronounce a curse—may it come on him.
He found no pleasure in blessing—may it be far from him.
He wore cursing as his garment;
it entered into his body like water, into his bones like oil.
May it be like a cloak wrapped about him,
like a belt tied forever around him.
May this be the LORD's payment to my accusers,
to those who speak evil of me.
Psalm 109:6-20 (Today's New International Version)

Our LORD, punish the Edomites!
Because the day Jerusalem fell, they shouted,
"Completely destroy the city! Tear down every building!"
Babylon, you are doomed!
I pray the Lord's blessings on anyone who punishes you
for what you did to us.
May the Lord bless everyone
who beats your children against the rocks!
Psalm 137:7-9 (Contemporary English Version)

These are harsh words. They call for vengeance without remorse or mercy. These words are so belligerent that John Wesley, perhaps the church's greatest theologian of love, recommended against ever reading these words in worship. It's not very hard to understand Wesley's hesitancy about reading psalms like these in church. These psalms heap curses upon the psalmist's enemies, oppressors and accusers; these prayers speak bluntly about the desire to see condemnation, hardship and devastation fall on adversaries. *These prayers exhibit no interest in curbing even the most extreme desires for retribution; they are violent and vindictive.* The psalmist even seeks God's blessing upon those who brutalize children! No words from Scripture are more shocking than this plea: "May the Lord bless everyone who beats your children against the rocks!"

These prayers—and a few others like them in the OT—were written by people who knew about victimization first hand. The Babylonians had surrounded Jerusalem, destroyed the city's walls and buildings, and demolished the temple. Hoards of Babylonian soldiers murdered all who resisted, and raped many who couldn't resist. The entire Jewish population had been terrorized, their homes looted and burnt. Many of the brutalized survivors were carried away for forced labor in unfamiliar lands. In the midst of these experiences—while still aching from the trauma of destruction, dislocation and death—some of those ancient exiles of Judah looked to Yahweh and uttered these pained and painful words.

For years, I struggled with these words. They obviously fail to model the forgiveness taught and practiced by Christ. I knew that such psalms should be read against the historical backdrop of the Babylonians' destruction of Jerusalem and Judah's subsequent exile in Babylon. But still, *I found little use for such hateful words*. That all changed one January day.

On that cold Boston day, I sat in my office and listened to a young lady explain to me how she had been beaten, raped, and left naked in a public park by an unknown assailant. We sobbed together. After several deep breaths—and with a quiet and dignified composure—she said, "Prof, I don't want to go to church and praise God. And I don't want to go to counseling and forgive that guy." *I understood why she wasn't ready to offer praise to God or forgiveness to her attacker.* But I didn't know what to say. We sat in awkward silence. Finally, she said, "I want to kill him! What should I do?"

At that moment—because of that young woman's trauma and tears—I understood these psalms for the first time. I opened my Bible and read these prayers to her without comment. After I finished reading, with a new found strength, *the young lady said, "That's how I feel. That's what I want to say to God."*

I've never been victimized or traumatized like that young lady. However, her experience—and the experience of the ancient Judeans—has convinced me that *there may be times when all that we have to give God is our anger.* Now, I don't think that God wants us to stop there—just with anger. But, there are times when anger is the only sincere gift that we can give God. *In times like that, God can handle—perhaps even desires to hear—our outrage.* Even our most distasteful and remorseless utterances are more honoring to God— and more redemptive for us—than our most tight-lipped and uncommunicative silences. Redemption can begin with honest and unvarnished expressions of outrage. *When anger is all we have to voice, we should voice even that to God.* We may be amazed what God can do with the gift of our uncamouflaged rage.

Lord, do not allow me to hide myself from you.

Elijah's Death Wish

"I've had enough, LORD," Elijah said. "Take my life; I'm no better than my ancestors."
Then he laid down under the tree and fell asleep.
1 Kings 19:4-5

Many times, I can read a prayer and not give a thought to how the person looked when he or she prayed the prayer. Not so with this prayer! *When I read Elijah telling God that he'd had enough, my mind's eye sees Elijah slumped over and emotionally collapsed.* Elijah was drained, depleted and ready to give up. I can almost hear Elijah bellow an exasperated half-moan, half-growl as he paused between calling upon the Lord's name on the one hand and asking God to take his life on the other hand.

Elijah had good reason to feel disillusioned. He'd been under a royal death sentence for years. The king had officially labeled him a "troublemaker for Israel." Elijah was so unpopular with his fellow Jews that he spent more than three years hiding in the home of a Gentile widow. Now, another king was seeking his life.

To make matters worse, history also weighed on Elijah (his ancestors were also a dismal lot!). When Elijah looked back on things, here's what he saw: Adam and Eve ate the fruit. Cain killed Abel. By Noah's time, the thoughts of all humanity was evil—and that continually. Abraham and Sarah doubted. Their sons, Isaac and Ishmael, fought. Jacob and Esau connived against each other. Joseph's brothers tried to murder him before they sold him into slavery.

After the exodus, the people rebelled against Moses and began worshipping a golden calf. In the time of Joshua, Gideon, Deborah, and the rest of the judges, the people's obedience was equally hit-and-miss. Then the paranoid King Saul tried to kill David. The adulterous David committed murder. The exploitative and indulgent Solomon took foreign wives by the hundreds. In Elijah's own time, God's people had broken into two separate and competing peoples, Judah and Israel.

When Elijah surveyed this history, he saw the rebelliousness, disobedience and ineffectiveness of God's people. History gave Elijah little basis for optimism. *Humanity's prognosis was bleak— and Elijah was no exception to the human condition.* Elijah had come to understand that he was no better than his ancestors.

It's pretty easy to be successful. We can be gracious and cheerful in our victories. We can be kind and generous—perhaps even self-effacing—while our accomplishments accumulate. In fact, when we're successful, we sometimes imagine that our gracious and kind dispositions distinguish us from the less noble masses. Most of us can handle success well; it's failure—or at least perceived failure—that really tests us. That's where Elijah was when he offered this prayer. He felt like a pretty undistinguished failure—and he wanted to die. He would rather be dead than be average.

Elijah forgot two important things. First, *not being superior is not the same thing as being a failure.* Elijah didn't misjudge his own capacities—he was no better than his ancestors. Elijah misjudged the significance of his capacities—being a person of typical capacities is no reason for dismay. Most of us are average. We're no smarter, no more insightful, and no more capable than most other people. Second, *it's okay to be non-exceptional, because it's not about us, it's about God.* In the wake of Elijah's foolish prayer for death, God reminded Elijah that he was not alone. God had 7000 prophets who had never bowed their knees to Baal. God was working through a whole host of people to accomplish God's purposes. Our individual callings and labors are significant and important, but they are only a small part of what God is doing.

Most people pass through seasons of disillusionment—even seasons of despondency. Such emotions can prompt us to make foolish utterances to God—just as Elijah did. When you pass through such times, don't beat yourself up or focus upon your perceived failures. Don't even ask God to make you more successful. Instead, focus upon the faithfulness of God and upon your call to live

86

faithfully in the sometimes small role you play in God's redemptive drama.

Lord, exhaust me so that I may find your strength.

Lament

Look, O LORD, and consider: Whom have you ever treated like this?
Should women eat their offspring, the children they have cared for?
Should priest and prophet be killed in the sanctuary of the Lord?
Young and old lie together in the dust of the streets;
my young men and maidens have fallen by the sword.
You have slain them in the day of your anger; you have slaughtered
them without pity.
As you summon to a feast day, so you summoned against me terrors
on every side.
In the day of the LORD's anger no one escaped or survived;
those I cared for and reared, my enemy has destroyed.
Lamentations 2:20-22 (New International Version)

This prayer opens with three questions. The first question can't be answered—no one can explain why the righteous suffer. The second and third questions are easily answered—parents shouldn't consume their own children and the servants of God shouldn't be murdered. The rest of the prayer catalogues the tragedies that accompanied *the Babylonian destruction of Jerusalem.* Men and women, the young and the old, were butchered by invading armies. Terror intruded on every area of life; death hovered in the air. *A few people survived, but no one truly escaped.* The experience was all-encompassing.

This prayer is both depressing and refreshing. It's depressing in the same way that tragedy, violence and loss are always depressing. But the prayer is refreshing in an entirely different way. This lament refreshes with its candor. *It dares to voice commonly felt—but seldom spoken—emotions.* Sadness rolls over all of us from time to time. We lose loved ones, we see suffering, and we are saturated by waves of sadness, loneliness, and dismay. *We hurt because we love.* When we see suffering, we ache in sympathy with the wounds of those we love. *The greater our love, the greater our pain.*

This prayer expresses the pain that comes from such love. We live in a world of pain. We hear the stories every day. A toddler drowns in the family pool. A teenage athlete succumbs to leukemia. A marriage is violated. Such pain issues from a thousand sources... senseless crimes, broken vows, crippling diseases, fractured relationships, substance abuse, lost children... *Broken-heartedness is the cost of genuine love; lament is the language of broken-hearted love.*

Christian life and worship must make room for lament and its outcries of pain and distress. *Lament should not disrupt our worship like an uninvited guest or undesired intruder. Without lament—and its emphatic declarations of the destructive power of sin—the celebration of grace is hollow.* Lament is the sorrow of Good Friday that gives legitimacy to the joyful expressions of Easter morning. In the absence of heart-rending laments, ongoing praise can sound little better than an incessant background hum. We offer praise because we have found grace in spite of our broken-heartedness. We celebrate because we understand that sin—with all of its mournful devastation—has been defeated.

We must not proclaim what one of my friends calls the gospel of emotional prosperity. *If you participate in the love of Jesus Christ, you will not be happy all the time. You will understand the sentiments of the savior who sweat blood over the sin of the world.* You will cry with Mary and Martha, you will weep over sinful Jerusalem, you will lament.

Learn to lament, and learn to allow others to lament—not because you do not believe in God's conquest of death, hell and the grave, but because you share God's sorrow over the havoc that sin brings into our world.

Lord, express your sorrows through me.

Prayer to the Idols

All who make idols are nothing, and the things they delight in do not profit; their witnesses neither see nor know. And so they will be put to shame. Who would fashion a god or cast an image that can do no good? Look, all its devotees shall be put to shame; the artisans too are merely human. Let them all assemble, let them stand up; they shall be terrified, they shall all be put to shame.
The blacksmith fashions it and works it over the coals, shaping it with hammers, and forging it with his strong arm; he becomes hungry and his strength fails, he drinks no water and is faint. The carpenter stretches a line, marks it out with a stylus, fashions it with planes, and marks it with a compass; he makes it in human form, with human beauty, to be set up in a shrine. He cuts down cedars or chooses a cypress tree or an oak and lets it grow strong among the trees of the forest. He plants a cedar and the rain nourishes it. Then it can be used as fuel. Part of it he takes and warms himself; he kindles a fire and bakes bread. Then he makes a god and worships it, makes it a carved image and bows down before it. Half of it he burns in the fire; over this half he roasts meat, eats it, and is satisfied. He also warms himself and says, 'Ah, I am warm, I can feel the fire!' The rest of it he makes into a god, his idol, bows down to it, and worships it; **he prays to it and says, 'Save me, for you are my god!'**
They do not know, nor do they comprehend; for their eyes are shut, so that they cannot see, and their minds as well, so that they cannot understand. No one considers, nor is there knowledge or discernment to say, 'Half of it I burned in the fire; I also baked bread on its coals, I roasted meat and have eaten. Now shall I make the rest of it an abomination? Shall I fall down before a block of wood?' He feeds on ashes; a deluded mind has led him astray, and **he cannot save himself or say, 'Is not this thing in my right hand a fraud?'**
Isaiah 44:12-20 (Revised Standard Version)

After listening to so many moving Christian and Jewish prayers over the last month, I have chosen to end our month together by considering this foolish pagan prayer. Isaiah's spoofing attitude intrigues me. I've always assumed that Isaiah's sarcastic rhetoric and satirical wit probably struck home with his audience. The common sense of Isaiah's observations certainly rings true today even though most of us have never encountered literal idolatry. Lest we forget... *we have the luxury of reading these words and presuming their truthfulness only because Isaiah possessed the moral courage to challenge the ancient world's ubiquitous idolatry.*

What becomes self-evident truth—like the truth that Isaiah spoke all those centuries ago—often comes to us at a great price. Tradition holds that Isaiah was sawed in half in a log. Isaiah's sacrifice fills just one line on one page in the very long book of the saints who have suffered for the truth. *Those who reject the idolatries of their day often find themselves speaking undesired truths. Such people may be called to lay down their lives; they will be called to sacrifice.*

We live in an age of tolerance and acceptance. Few of us would denigrate a proclivity for civility or a tendency toward empathy. However, there is an all important difference between tolerance and indifference, and between acceptance and disregard. When we truly care about people, we speak the truth to them. Refusing to wear your seat belt endangers your life; smoking will probably shorten your life; extramarital sex will not make you happier. These things are true whether you believe them or not. It would not be tolerant or accepting of me to refrain from telling you these things simply because you refused to believe them. The restraint of truth is no virtue. *An unwillingness to speak the truth does not demonstrate an acceptance and valuing of the other. In fact, such complicity with falsehood entails a profound devaluing and rejection of the other.*

Two truths from Isaiah: First, *we cannot fashion (or refashion) God to fit our whims.* Social scientists have observed an interesting phenomenon over the years. Those who worship idols

91

tend to create idols that look just like themselves. *Idolators make idols in their own image.* That's the appeal of idolatry. You can make God into whatever you want God to be. Of course, what you whittle out of the log is no more significant or powerful or divine than the surplus wood shavings scattered at your feet. The God revealed in Scripture has a unique personality, an individual volition, and a redemptive mission that cannot be altered to comply with our personal whims. Not even the most culturally appealing refashioning or reshaping of that divine character can be true or tolerated. God wishes to remake us in the divine image, and God will not allow us to remake God in our image.

Even when you worship a fraud sincerely, you're still worshipping a fraud. Many people today think that it doesn't matter what you believe as long as you believe it sincerely. Few things could be further from the truth. *A false hope is worse than no hope. Sincere people can be wrong.* Sincere people can highjack planes and bomb terrified masses. In our culture, many people are satisfied with any type of "spirituality." *But spirituality is not Christianity. It matters to whom you pray.* As Christians, we do not pray to a generic, one size fits all, man upstairs or to some universal spirit of good will. Sincerity alone offers no protection against fraud. We pray to a very specific Being, to our Creator and Sustainer, to the God revealed in the cross and resurrection of Jesus Christ.

Lord, you and you alone are God. There is none beside you.

Afterword

Prayer is not like an IRS audit. You do not need to worry about what you say. You don't need to be on your guard against saying the wrong thing. God already knows what you really think, so there's no need to be defensive and no value in being deceptive. Pray. Pray aloud. Pray silently. Pray in writing. Pray alone. Pray in groups. Pray however you want. Pray in whatever manner you wish. But pray... and pray honestly.

There are no good and bad prayers. Prayer is simply conversation with a friend who sticks closer than any other friend or brother or sister. Speak to God as you would speak to your best friend, to your doctor, to your spouse, to your parent, to your boss, to your Creator, to your Savior. Your relationship with God can be as intimate and multi-faceted as all the rest of your relationships combined.

At this point, I have only *two pieces of advice.* I've already offered the *first—pray often and honestly.* Never give God the silent treatment out of fear, shame or discontent. And never allow the hectic pace of life completely crowd out the God who is frantic to talk with you. If nothing else, give God the tatters and scraps of time around the edges of your day. *Second, be attentive to overhear the prayers of others.* Learn from the interaction of God's other friends and family members. Use and reuse the prayers in this book, or search the Scriptures and the Christian Tradition for other prayers. But learn to overhear the prayers of the saints. You're not in this alone. The walk of faith is a marathon with a great cloud of witnesses.

I close with a request. If you write out some prayers, send them to me and let me overhear them. I like to overhear the prayers of the saints (yes, there's more saintliness in you than you realize).